DON'T GIVE UP
UNTIL YOU DO

About the Author

Fred H. Meyer, MD (Fort Collins, CO) is a retired physician and long-time practitioner of Shambhala Buddhism. Throughout his thirty-five years of practice, he has studied with many of the most respected Buddhist teachers. He is a founding member of the Fort Collins Shambhala Center and the Chögyam Trungpa Center, where he has taught in residence for the past decade.

To Write to the Author

If you wish to contact the author or would like more information about this book, please write to the author in care of Llewellyn Worldwide, and we will forward your request. Both the author and publisher appreciate hearing from you and learning of your enjoyment of this book and how it has helped you. Llewellyn Worldwide cannot guarantee that every letter written to the author can be answered, but all will be forwarded. Please write to:

Fred H. Meyer
℅ Llewellyn Worldwide
2143 Wooddale Drive
Woodbury, MN 55125-2989

Please enclose a self-addressed stamped envelope for reply, or $1.00 to cover costs. If outside the USA, enclose an international postal reply coupon.

DON'T GIVE UP UNTIL YOU DO

❂ ———————————————— ❂

From Mindfulness to Realization
on the Buddhist Path

❂ ———————————————— ❂

FRED H. MEYER, MD

Llewellyn Publications
Woodbury, Minnesota

FIRST EDITION
First Printing, 2012

Book design by Bob Gaul
Editing by Laura Graves
Cover design by Ellen Lawson
Cover art © Sky and tree: iStockphoto.com/David Schrader

Llewellyn Publications is a registered trademark of Llewellyn Worldwide Ltd.

Library of Congress Cataloging-in-Publication Data
Meyer, Fred H., 1941–
   Don't give up until you do: from mindfulness to realization on the Buddhist
path/Fred H. Meyer. —1st ed.
      p. cm.
   Includes bibliographical references.
   ISBN 978-0-7387-3284-8
1. Meditation—Buddhism. 2. Buddhism—Doctrines. I. Title.
   BQ5612.M49 2012
   294.3'4435—dc23
                       2012012810

Llewellyn Worldwide Ltd. does not participate in, endorse, or have any authority
or responsibility concerning private business transactions between our authors and
the public.
   All mail addressed to the author is forwarded, but the publisher cannot, unless
specifically instructed by the author, give out an address or phone number.
   Any Internet references contained in this work are current at publication time,
but the publisher cannot guarantee that a specific location will continue to be
maintained. Please refer to the publisher's website for links to authors' websites and
other sources.

Llewellyn Publications
A Division of Llewellyn Worldwide Ltd.
2143 Wooddale Drive
Woodbury, MN 55125-2989
www.llewellyn.com

Printed in the United States of America

This book is dedicated with love and appreciation to my son, Frederick. His editing, interactions with the publisher, and support of me and the book were indispensable. I will always cherish memories of the intelligence, gentleness, and kindness he extended toward his father as well as others during the lengthy process of writing the book and bringing it to the public.

Contents

Introduction

We all have a mind, and mind is both what experiences realization and what is realized, so we all have everything we need to attain the highest levels of insight.

Since the time of the Buddha, committed meditators have told of a state that is the pinnacle of human experience— the state of realization. Although words could only approximate their experience, they still did their best to share it with others. In this book, an account of my own experiences over thirty-five years as a Buddhist practitioner, I too have attempted to present the pith and glory of the Buddhist path, from the initial cultivation of mindfulness to the realization of the true nature of mind and reality.

I was introduced to Buddhism in my mid-thirties, while practicing medicine in Minneapolis. My first exposure was to the Zen Buddhist teachings, and, steeped as I was in Western thought, I found their perspective both unique and arcane. My interest led me to read several books by the noted Zen authors Alan Watts and D. T. Suzuki, books that I found for the most part incomprehensible. Driven by curiosity as well as chronic psychological pain, I eventually sought out a local Zen teacher, Dainin Katagiri Roshi, who introduced me to meditation in 1975.

For three years after meeting Roshi, I sporadically read and practiced the Dharma, or Buddhist way. Then, in a time of great stress, I spontaneously saw that no self, ego, or central entity was guiding my life—a landmark insight on the Buddhist path. This breakthrough prompted me to intensify my study and practice, and to read a book called *The Myth of Freedom* by the Tibetan teacher Chögyam Trungpa Rinpoche. I did not expect that I would soon encounter him, and his world, firsthand.

Chögyam Trungpa Rinpoche, my teacher, appears often in this book. As the eleventh holder of the Trungpa Tulku lineage, he excelled as a scholar, meditation master, teacher, poet, artist, and world-renowned author. He also founded Vajradhatu, an international group of Buddhist centers; Shambhala Training, a worldwide secular approach to enlightenment; and Naropa University, the first contemplative university in the new world. As impressive as those accomplishments are, he was more distinguished in my eyes as a teacher who embodied enlightenment and transmitted it to others. (I relate many of my experiences with him in another book, *In the Buddha's Realm: A Physician's Experiences with Chögyam Trungpa, a Modern-Day Buddha.*)

After meeting Chögyam Trungpa Rinpoche, I put my career as an academic physician on hold and moved to Karmê Chöling, a Buddhist meditation center in Vermont that he directed. I lived there for two and a half years, after which I reentered medicine, practicing in Colorado as an internist and rheumatologist until my retirement in 2009. Throughout this time, I continued my journey on the Buddhist path, attending Rinpoche in Boulder, Colorado, until his death in 1987. Later, I assisted his son, Sakyong Mipham Rinpoche, the head of Shambhala International. Through the years, the combination of appropriate teachers, teachings, and practices, as well as the stress of caring for patients—which proved a powerful stimulus to progress on the path—allowed me to see for myself, in myself, the truth of the Buddhist teachings. That truth is the source of these writings.

The pivotal truth in Buddhism, and a pivotal term in this book, is realization. Realization is the experience of the empty, aware nature of mind. Realization and enlightenment refer to the same level of insight, but the two terms are not synonymous. According to Tulku Urgyen, a great twentieth-century Tibetan teacher, realization does not become enlightenment until the mind never strays from what it has realized.

When we experience realization, we literally gain nothing: we awaken to our true nature, which is nothing. Although the nothing is vast, restful, blissful, and vividly aware, it is still nothing. We gain nothing in another sense, as well, because realization isn't anything we acquire or add on; in fact, it occurs only when everything that obscures it is removed. This is the reason why spiritual credentials can be self-defeating. We can accumulate a lot on a spiritual journey: the extensive knowledge we have acquired, the great teachers we have met, the holy sites we have visited—the list goes on, and attaching to any entry in that list inhibits us from discovering the nothingness we really are. Every credential we gain is another link in the golden chain of spirituality: pleasant to wear and display, but still a chain, shackling us to our sense of being someone. As a physician, I have spent countless hours advising patients to give up things that harm them, at least as much time as I have spent actively rescuing them from harm. Spirituality is the same way: to realize true spirituality, we must give up the many things we believe we are.

Experiencing realization is not easy. In fact, it is one of the most difficult things we could endeavor to do, because in truth it can't be done—it happens spontaneously under the correct circumstances. In part because of this difficulty, Buddhist practitioners rarely give personal accounts of their realization experiences, since this invites both skepticism and the perception that they may be seeking attention. This book is less reserved on the subject. The fruitions of Buddhism are as crucial as the teachings and practices that lead to them, and should be discussed as openly. Furthermore, one of the book's major purposes is to *democratize* realization, to show that regular people like you and me can attain it; that it is not the exclusive province of the robed, titled, or "chosen," as many people believe. We all have a mind, and mind is both what experiences realization and what is realized, so we all have everything we need to attain the highest levels of insight.

I have tried to present the material in this book simply and clearly, using everyday language in lieu of technical Buddhist terminology when possible. I have also tried to vivify the insights presented here with accounts of my life as a person in the world, a practicing physician, and a traveler on the spiritual path. Readers will learn what realization is, what it feels like, the stages leading to it, the methods for attaining it, and pitfalls to be avoided, in what I hope is an interesting and enjoyable presentation. The intent is always to stimulate readers into experiencing for themselves the truths described here.

I will stop here, and formally—but not too formally—welcome you to this book. Although what I say does not differ from what the Buddha or those who followed him said, I hope that presenting these truths in a fresh, direct, and unique way will stimulate your interest in realization and accelerate your progress toward it. If that happens, writing this book will have been worth the effort.

Awareness

---

*Since we are aware, we know there is awareness—
we can hear, see, taste, smell, and touch. But if we look
for what allows us to do these things, we will be unable to
find it. We may be able to locate our sensory organs, but
the mind receiving their messages eludes us.*

In everyday usage, the term "awareness" suggests that we apply "our" awareness to something else. We might hear, "I'm aware of the problem," or, "You should be aware of what you're doing," implying that one entity is focusing its awareness on another.

This is not the way awareness feels in realization. (I use the word "feel," because one *feels* the qualities of realization rather than intellectually knowing or understanding them.) Instead, awareness feels like it has no owner—self-existing, its own entity, much as we experience snow. People don't say, "They made a nice snow today." Similarly, in realization, awareness feels like part of the atmosphere and not anyone's creation. If we experience it in this way, we can relax and allow it to work on its own, which is how it works best.

There is a little test that proves awareness is self-existing and not our creation. Bankei, a great Zen teacher whom I love, used it often in his teachings. To perform the test, sit quietly in a tidy room without any distractions, and just be aware of your breathing. While doing this, you will eventually begin to notice sounds around you, such as traffic, birds, or barking dogs. Now reflect: did *you* try to hear those sounds, or did awareness, without your supervision, hear them on its own? This is not a trick—I am appealing to your experience. Did you make an effort to hear all those sounds, or did they become known to awareness without any effort on your part? If you look closely, you will see that awareness is indeed self-existing, and not something you or anyone else creates.

In realization, awareness never feels as though it is inside or outside of us. To appreciate this, we must experience another aspect of reality called nonduality. We realize nonduality when the barrier dissolves between what we conceptualize as inside and outside. No longer divided, awareness is then felt to be everywhere, limitless—or, as it is sometimes described in Buddhist texts, extending throughout limitless space.

In addition to being self-existing, nondual, and vast, awareness has another quality that may seem strange: it is not aware of anything in particular. It never fixates; to do so would contradict its free, self-existing nature. Although it can distinguish "a hawk from a handsaw" (to quote Hamlet), that is one of its lesser attributes.

Awareness as experienced in realization is like a mirror. It makes no attempt to see or reflect things, but simply observes passively. It never selects some images and rejects others; and since it doesn't categorize or fixate on anything, all objects appear the same to it, even though it can still distinguish between them. A fitting word to describe the sameness experienced in realization is "That," with a capital "T"—not as in "that horse" or "that plane," but simply That. Anyone can appreciate this experience: everyone's first visual perception of an object, before assigning a label to it, is That. With the insight of realization, however, objects *remain* as That, because one's perceptions no longer change immediately into ego-generated concepts about them.

Also, self-existing awareness does not exist as a thing. Since we are aware, we know there is awareness—we can hear, see, taste, smell, and touch. But if we look for what allows us to do these things, we will be unable to find it. We may be able to locate our sensory organs, but the mind receiving their messages eludes us. This inability to find anything is a characteristic of emptiness, a something (or nothing) that is inseparable from awareness, and a topic we will discuss later.

I should mention that the Buddhist practitioner's experience of awareness develops in stages. The qualities of awareness described above will probably feel like big epiphanies when we first experience them, but our lives will also be filled with smaller—but still important—epiphanies, such as the one that follows.

In my early forties, I took what eventually became a three-year hiatus from medicine to gain a broader sense of the world. In other words, I was having a midlife crisis, compounded (I would later understand) by major depression. I had studied and practiced Zen Buddhism intermittently, but after quitting my job, I moved to Austin, Texas and began meditating intensively.

Being divorced and lonely, I welcomed the chance to meet women. One morning after practicing meditation I walked to a park, where I encountered an attractive woman. I began my mating ritual: talking rapidly to show off my intelligence and wit, while dropping the fact that I was a physician. This time, however, meditation allowed me to see the effects of my display, and the glimpse I received wasn't pretty: she was looking at me with a mixture of confusion and alarm, while trying to assess my sanity. Realizing that I was a turkey no matter what my plumage, I murmured a few embarrassed words and left. I had just taken a step toward greater awareness.

LOVE

Love is not meant to be aimed at a specific target, like a gun. True love is a state of being, not something one does to—I'm tempted to say "inflicts upon"—another.

It's getting close to Christmas, so it seems a good time to talk about love. I have spent a lot of time discussing spirituality with both Buddhists and non-Buddhists, and find that non-Buddhists, in particular, make much of love.

Many of us fit love to our needs. We can even be persuaded to speak of it as universal and not directed toward anything in particular, which is often a far cry from how we apply it in our everyday lives. When not pressed, though, we are more likely to view love as do the young people who rhapsodize about it: as a many-splendored thing involving a specific other and often tainted by a whiff of possessiveness. (I have read my share of these rhapsodies in poetry forums.) Some truckers I worked with as a youth once told me that the problem with young people was that they didn't know the difference between being in love and in heat. Reading young people's poetry has helped me, in my old age, to understand what those great philosophers meant.

Love is much abused, not least by its double use as a noun and a verb. From a Buddhist standpoint, love fares beautifully as a noun, but suffers greatly as a verb. Love is not meant to be aimed at a specific target, like a gun. True love is a state of being, not something one does to—I'm tempted to say "inflicts upon"—another. Using love as a verb also means that "oneself" must bring it to bear upon a putative "other." This presents a real problem in Buddhism, where self and other do not exist. Love's limitations as a verb are apparent in one of the most misleading phrases in English: "I love you." That phrase contains a hornet's nest of misinformation, equal to "I think, therefore I am" (wherein Descartes first blindly accepts what he proposes to prove—that "I" exists—then asserts incorrectly that "I" thinks, then asserts, also incorrectly, that the act of thinking proves the existence of a thinker).

A failure as a verb, love works much better as a noun. In and of themselves, nouns don't do anything; they just lay around being. As my teacher Chögyam Trungpa used to say about a number of things, authentic love is "radiation without a radiator." In this regard, it is similar to compassion, the preferred word in Buddhism, since we don't "compassion" others. (One will hear reputable Buddhist teachers use the term "love," however, so it is not excluded from Buddhism.)

Although I may appear critical of love, it comes immediately to mind as a description of my devotion to Chögyam Trungpa. I practice Vajrayana Buddhism, the third *yana* ("path" or "vehicle") in Buddhism along with the Hinayana and Mahayana. The Vajrayana is the yana of devotion. Its practices and insights are based on devotion toward one's teacher, who is regarded as enlightenment in human form. Without devotion, the Vajrayana remains "self-secret": completely inaccessible.

Devotion in Tibetan is *mögu: möpa* means "longing" and *gupa* means "humbleness." The combination of these two qualities, longing and humbleness, constitute the Vajrayana sense of devotion. Having been a Vajrayana practitioner for thirty years, I am familiar with the teachings on devotion, but the concepts of longing and humbleness for a long time failed to connect me with a strong sense of it. It took love to do that. When I finally understood what my teacher represented, my devotion arose as love, and it has remained that way. That insight has ushered me into the magic of the Vajrayana, and opened me to love both in a general sense as well as specifically toward others.

We all know the wonders of love, but this marvelous experience, like so many other aspects of life, is often polluted by ego. Love can be egoless, as we see every day in the self-sacrifice of parents for their children, spouses for each other, and in the world at large. I respect love—how could I not when it is the word that best expresses my devotion to my teacher? Nevertheless, I am always careful not to taint it with attachment.

Body

---

*No one or thing inhabits our bodies. Having this
perspective allows us to make better decisions about body,
because the space or distance created by non-ownership
establishes a more accurate and balanced approach to it.*

Let's talk about body. Body can be approached from both
a confused and a realized perspective. The confused experience of body is that it belongs to us; in fact, it is our most
prized possession. This attitude makes sense, because without realization we may believe that when the body dies we
do as well.

The sense that we possess our bodies leads to many of
the same lopsided attitudes toward them as we take toward
our other possessions. As a physician, I see these attitudes
and the dangers they pose. A common one with men is
ignorance. Many men feel it is not "manly" to care for their
bodies, and that only sissies go running to the doctor. Like

soldiers in war, they adopt a fatalistic attitude: "When my time is up, I'll die." The worst of these types, in my experience, are American Indians. Those I have cared for have had a total disregard for their bodies, and I must admit I respect them for their courage, if not their longevity.

Then there is the group who protects their bodies to excess, running to the doctor with minor problems whenever their insurance allows. They fear death, and feel that every twinge portends the beginning of the end. This and the ignorant approach form the two poles of the many neurotic ways people approach their bodies.

Strong attachment to body creates excessive fear if something affects it. This fear in itself may lead to problems worse than the body's ills. For example, patients in pain may overstate their pain because of fear, leading their physicians to overmedicate them; this is one reason for the booming narcotic prescription problem in America. Patients begin with pain amplified by fear, and end up adding on narcotic dependency or addiction.

In realization, body is seen to be without owner. A Chán (Chinese Zen) teacher once brought a student to realization by asking, "Who is it who drags your corpse around?" The student, having the presence of mind to look for the answer, found no one. Voilà!

No one or thing inhabits our bodies. Having this perspective allows us to make better decisions about body, because the space or distance created by nonownership establishes a more accurate and balanced approach to it. Body's problems cause less panic and irrationality, allowing us to better evaluate its true condition.

Buddha made clear in his teachings that although body isn't ours, it is important. He said, "Without body, there is no Dharma." (*Dharma* is a Sanskrit word meaning "truth" or "norm," and refers both to the truth Buddha discovered and to the Buddhist teachings.) Suicide is eschewed in Buddhism, because there is no Dharma when we die, and because we are all potential buddhas: each of us has a mind that, when liberated from confusion, is that of a buddha. Since we have the potential to attain buddhahood in this lifetime, killing ourselves is an egregious act.

Many people believe that mind dies with their bodies, but realization corrects this misimpression. Realization brings the insight that mind is self-existing, and one of the ramifications of this insight is that mind doesn't die when the body does, for the simple reason that it doesn't belong to body. When we experience the true nature of mind, it will *feel* like it exists on its own and not as a creation of body. That feeling is the basis for the understanding that mind continues when we die, one of the foundations of the Buddhist principle of reincarnation.

Similarly, we may wonder why dead people have no mind. If we think it's because their brains are dead and they can no longer create mind, we are mistaken: the experience of mind in realization is not one of creating mind, but of receiving it. With this experience, it makes sense that at the time of death mind continues in the world, since only its receiver and not itself ceases.

We all have a very strong attachment to body. Of all the things we must learn to give up in the Dharma, body is the most difficult. However, great benefit results if we can see that body is not really ours. This will be especially true when Yama, the Lord of Death, comes calling.

SILENCE

---

*The beauty of silence, besides the exquisite
restfulness it provides, is that it affords a
means for connecting with realized mind.*

I belong to a spiritual poetry forum on the Internet. One
of the regulars in this group goes by Narinder and hails
from India. Narinder is a nice guy, but a somewhat impen-
etrable poet: he uses a lot of "aums" and other gesticula-
tions in his poetry, so reading it can be challenging. At any
rate, Narinder's poetry speaks of silence, a topic I never paid
much attention until recently, when I had a rather powerful
insight: mind is silent.

Most of us who have observed mind through meditation or otherwise would say that it is anything but quiet,
since it is filled with a steady chatter of strung-together
thoughts, unrelated words and half-words, songs, and occa-
sional emotional tsunamis. Mind's silence is only understood

when the source of the chatter—realized mind—is accessed. It is in realization that one hears the velvety silence of mind; and once experienced, the silence is so prominent that it can be used as an indicator of having reached that state of mind.

One never knows where the Buddhist path will lead. All the major insights I have experienced have been totally surprising to me, although experiencing them usually calls to mind associations with what I had previously heard or read. Such was the case with silence: I remembered Narinder speaking of silence (amongst the aums), and Chögyam Trungpa referring to "silent living" as an aspect of realization.

Surprisingly, I can't remember silence having been mentioned in any Buddhist literature I have read. Realized mind has many well-documented attributes—among them emptiness, awareness, vastness, unbornness, unceasingness, nondwellingness, compassion, restfulness, freedom, and vividness—but, at least from my own reading, not silence. Obviously, Narinder knows of the silence of mind, as did my teacher. I suppose the lack of writing on silence makes sense, considering how little I now find to say about it other than that mind is indeed silent.

When one first experiences realization, in some sense the work has just begun. Only in enlightenment does one permanently remain there; before that, one must find ways to transition to it from everyday mind. The beauty of silence, besides the exquisite restfulness it provides, is that it affords a means for connecting with realized mind. Admittedly, I have found probably twenty such entry points to realization through the years, and something may yet arrive that displaces silence. Right now, though, it is my mediator of choice.

I also find that my experience of the silence of mind is highlighted by sounds in the environment. A Zen story supports the existence of this avenue to understanding. A monk had been sitting in solitary meditation for a long time in a hut, when one day someone began sweeping outside. By chance, the sweeper flicked a stone against the door of the hut, making a sharp sound. At the noise, the monk experienced the true nature of mind. I now suspect that the sound connected the monk with the silence of primordial mind. How wonderful it would be if every noise in our environment connected us to realization: we would then have a foolproof method for remaining in it. Unfortunately, that has not been the case with me, and I hesitate to encourage any willful attempt to use sounds in this way, since doing so could become an ego-generating activity.

I am also happy to report that Simon and Garfunkel were right: I now know that silence has sound. That song title always seemed like pseudo-Buddhism to me, but with my discovery I have found silence to have an aural quality as palpable as conventional sounds. In fact, after first experiencing the silence of mind, this quality was so vivid that I considered meditating and living in its soothing tone forever. Maybe someday I will, while I read Narinder's poetry.

First Spiritual
Experience

The true meaning of Christmas, love and forgiveness,
stays with me from the days when struggling alone
I discovered what Christ represented.

Today is Christmas. Although I am a Buddhist, I celebrated the holiday with my wife and son. We decorated a tree ("Buddha Bush"), exchanged presents, and later went horseback riding. It proved a wonderful day, especially for me, who has a long past of sordid Christmases. I do not wish to seem maudlin, but the fact is that my youth and most of its Christmases were marred by dysfunctional parents. I find it a relief, and amusing, that I enjoy Christmases more as a Buddhist than I ever did as a Catholic.

Every situation has a positive and negative side. At the age of seven, I was bundled off to St. Joseph's Junior Military

School, a boarding school run by nuns, where I lived for six years. The experience at St. Joseph's was hideous, and I still suffer from the psychological and physical abuse I received there. (Yes, nuns can be physically abusive if you are a small child and live with them.) This dark cloud had a silver lining, however, for the years of misery I endured led me to an early spiritual experience.

I was probably around eleven when it happened. Out of loneliness, I began playing sexually with a boy in the dorm bed next to me (this is not uncommon for lonely boys), and another boy reported me to the nuns. When a nun confronted me, the combination of her vehemence, my belief that I had sinned against God, and my lack of parental support generated intense stress in me. The natural person for me to turn to, and the one the nuns always recommended, was Jesus. One day, while praying to Jesus for help, I had a sudden transformative experience: I felt he had forgiven me, which filled me with relief and flooded me with love. A sense of freedom and airiness entered my being. It was not realization, but it showed me at an early age that alternatives to everyday mind existed. I believe to this day that my childhood epiphany with Jesus prepared my mind for the insights I would later have in Buddhism.

Jesus was my first spiritual experience—not as a person who actually loved and helped me, but as a representation that such energy or spirit existed in the world. I still love Jesus to this day, and I would be happy to tell anyone, Buddhist or otherwise, of that love. Despite all the dark associations I have,

Christmas and the birth of Christ still remind me of my first spiritual insight.

Success in anything arises from nature and nurture. We may excel in something because of innate ability, prolonged experience, or both. If we start swinging a golf club at age six, chances are that we will eventually become a good golfer; and if we have good physical and mental endowment, we may become a champion. I believe the same is true of mind. People have aptitudes for realization like everything else, and if they experience a mental breakthrough early in life, their chances for further breakthroughs improve.

In Tibet, gurus are taken to monasteries at an early age and trained. In his book *Born in Tibet,* Chögyam Trungpa describes being chosen by a guru and trained from an early age to optimize his chances for spiritual success. Although my experience was different from my teacher's in many ways, in others it was similar. His childhood was stressful because of the high expectations others had of him, mine because of neglect; in both cases, however, the stress occurred in a religious setting and provided the foundation for our spirituality.

Although I have been a Buddhist for many years, Christmas still means something to me. The true meaning of Christmas, love and forgiveness, stays with me from the days when struggling alone I discovered what Christ represented. At a fortuitously early age, the spirit of Christ opened my mind. Although this experience resulted from the mistreatment of an innocent child, it nevertheless prepared that child for the wonders of Buddhism.

NOTHING

---

*To a large extent, what realized
people realize is Nothing.*

Nothing came to mind today. What could be better, since nothing is one of the many things I love?

I love nothing because it lies at the heart of the Dharma. If one can realize nothing, the rest of the Dharma is simply a refinement of that insight. This Nothing (capitalized to prevent confusion with the common usage) is not merely the absence of objects, but an experience with pleasing attributes, such as freedom and restfulness. Moreover, it is the source of all things. Everything arises from Nothing—not in the sense of being created by it, but of being complemented by it. There can be no form without formlessness: all form in the world, including all the activities of mind, exists in association with formlessness or Nothing, and this formlessness is so pervasive that in the experience of realization all phenomena appear to float in it. Buddhist Nothing is much more than the space between two trees: it is the space *of* the trees, inseparable from their form, as it is with all objects in the universe.

Unfortunately, Nothing is difficult to experience. In fact, the trouble of experiencing it is a major obstacle on the path to enlightenment, especially for anyone who approaches it through concept, since the Nothing of mind and reality cannot be arrived at logically.

Why is Nothing so difficult to experience? We can feel the absence of wealth (the "nothing" of money) quite acutely, so why is Nothing inaccessible when it presents as an aspect of reality itself? This problem arises partly because we have fixated so strongly on *things*—cars, faces, words, thoughts, emotions—that we are prevented from experiencing their counterpart, no-thing or Nothing. It is like dark matter in physics: scientists have been so fascinated by the stars and planets that they have failed to notice the unseen material existing in profusion around them.

Another problem is that Nothing is not readily apparent to the senses: we can see that an empty glass contains no water, but perceiving Nothing as contrasted to form is not so easy. In Buddhism, the term "emptiness" is preferred to "nothing" or "nothingness." "Nothing" presumes extinction, while emptiness, though not really providing much more as a concept, better illustrates the richness of the Buddhist experience of absence. At any rate, both words refer to the pith and glory of Buddhism, and to the basis of reality.

In fact, to a large extent, what realized people realize is Nothing: its presence (or absence) gives all phenomena their air of unreality and illusoriness, and it is what endows the mind of realization with the limitless space, rest, quiet, and surcease from struggle that confused mind lacks.

Unfortunately, reading about Nothing can be like having nothing in one's stomach: it creates hunger without providing a means to satisfy it. Having ideas and no experience is to "eat the menu for the meal," as they say in Zen. Descriptions of food do not fill bellies. Only when we give everything up, and our mind—prepared by the appropriate teacher, practices, and teachings—discovers the Nothing that is left, do we get our fill. That is when the dharmic feast, the delicious aspects of Nothing, is served.

Letting Go

---

*It is possible to have the whole card house of our
clinging collapse, to become so disappointed in our life
that all attachment is torn from our hearts in an instant.
That's the fast approach—fast and painful.*

I once saw a teacher demonstrate the whole path to enlightenment by making a fist and then slowly opening it. He was demonstrating letting go.

There are two aspects to letting go: knowing how to do it, and knowing what to let go. The first presents an immediate problem: if we try to let go, we are still trying and not letting go. This is a basic conundrum in Buddhism. What to do?

The answer is to place ourselves in a situation where we can give up without trying. Such a situation exists in meditation: sitting in an upright posture in a clean, quiet space and following our breath creates the perfect atmosphere for us to let go without trying. Unfortunately, very soon after beginning a meditation practice, we will find ourselves continuing to try—trying, for example, to stop our thoughts and emotions. Eventually, however, the practice itself solves this problem by teaching us how to relax. After expending large amounts of effort and many hours in meditation, we realize that thoughts and emotions are impossible to stop. When this happens, we give up trying to manipulate our mental activities and begin seeing them as simply phenomena with only the power to disturb us that we assign them. At that point we relax, and that is how we learn to give up without trying.

Meditation is the slow approach to giving up, but there is also a fast one. The fast one is to have our hearts broken so completely that we let go of all our obscurations to realization at once. It is possible to have the whole card house of our clinging collapse, to become so disappointed in our life that all attachment is torn from our hearts in an instant. That's the fast approach—fast and painful.

We probably have some idea of how to commit ourselves to meditation, but how do we go about getting our hearts broken? First, we need a heart, but not any old heart: we need one filled with courage, caring, an ethical approach to life, and a never-say-die attitude. Also, since we are too smart to place ourselves voluntarily in a situation where we will get our heart broken, it has to be broken by surprise. If we have the right heart, and especially if we have the right teacher, life will take care of that. At some point, usually with the teacher's orchestration, our heart will attach to some aspect of life, and then the object of our attachment will be jerked away. A breakthrough occurs: our heart breaks, and what is left in the rubble is realization.

One of the great Tibetan yogins was Milarepa, famous for his attainment in the Dharma. His teacher was Marpa the Translator, another renowned figure in eleventh-century Tibetan Buddhism. Marpa saw from the beginning that Milarepa had an exceptional potential for enlightenment, and he knew how to develop it. Since Milarepa was desperate for enlightenment, Marpa decided to use his desperation as a way to bring him to enlightenment.

Marpa did this by refusing to give Milarepa the teachings until he had built a stone house by hand. The work was brutal, and each time Milarepa would build a house, Marpa would tell him to tear it down, giving one or another spurious reason. As the work continued, Milarepa's back became a mass of bleeding tissue from carrying the stones. The process became so cruel that Marpa's wife could no longer tolerate Milarepa's suffering at the hands of her husband, and arranged for him to leave. Unfortunately, her kindness snatched enlightenment from Milarepa: after his departure, Marpa told his wife that if she had not interfered, Milarepa would very soon have attained enlightenment.

What can we gather from this story? Marpa had placed Milarepa on the fast path to letting go. He had made Milarepa build and tear down stone houses in the hope of breaking his heart, of getting him to finally and completely give up all his plans for receiving the teachings. He knew that when Milarepa's heart broke—and Milarepa had a huge heart: he was known as "the little man with the big heart"—he would experience the full truth of the Dharma.

If we want to let go, we should know what is going. Unfortunately, the Dharma doesn't work that way: we only discover what we let go of when it happens, because our concepts about life are so powerfully linked to us that we only notice them as they leave. In fact, to be told what we must let go of—"ego," "attachment to the phenomenal world," and so forth—can create further problems for us, because we may develop ideas about these things that are simply ideas and not the things themselves. We may try letting go of something that doesn't exist, something only in our imagination. Since we need to lose real things, it is in some sense better not to know what is to be lost and to allow ourselves to discover it by being processed through appropriate situations, like meditation on the slow path and a broken heart on the fast one.

I have discussed letting go, how to do it, and what to let go. I have also laid out the two approaches to it: meditation and heartbreak. However we approach it, though, letting go is not easy. Nothing worthwhile is.

THE FIRST PRINCIPLE

---

*As in all other endeavors, discipline is required on
the path to enlightenment; in fact, Chögyam Trungpa
once told us, "Discipline is my favorite word."*

In the thirty-five years I have practiced the Dharma, I have
found many helpful principles on the path to enlightenment.
One, however, overrides the rest: never give up. Amusing as
this may seem to readers with some understanding of the
importance of giving up in Buddhism, I am quite serious.

People do give up on the path. Some quit outright;
others may continue to identify themselves as Buddhists
and attend talks or read the Dharma, but they give up on
their own hearts and minds. They begin to believe that enlightenment is only for the few, the robed, the titled, and not
for them. They speak of the great attainment of So-And-So
Rinpoche, implying that no mere "person on the street"
could ever match it. They may lower their goals, deciding

that it is enough to be gentler, more aware, a little saner in this lifetime. They let themselves off the hook.

Others, feeling that they can't attain enlightenment, attempt to bring it to their level through intellectual games. They may reason (and espouse) that enlightenment is in everything, so there is no need to seek it. Or they may deny that it exists at all, asserting that anyone who claims to experience it is simply caught in another concept.

Finally, and most commonly, many people stop practicing meditation, cutting themselves off from the best chance they have of actually experiencing the Dharma. They stop being Dharma-doers and become Dharma-talkers.

In any endeavor, persistence is required. Woody Allen, the great spiritualist, once said that "Eighty percent of success is just showing up," and there is a lot of truth in that. Whatever we do, if we just keep doing it, we have an excellent chance for success. As in all other endeavors, discipline is required on the path to enlightenment; in fact, Chögyam Trungpa once told us, "Discipline is my favorite word." We may dream of the big spiritual breakthrough—the blinding light, like Saint Paul experienced on the road to Damascus—but for most of us that doesn't happen without the little daily breakthroughs discipline provides.

The Dharma is not easy. We often observe how we fail to fulfill its vision. No matter our level of experience, when we meditate we experience the capriciousness of mind, how our thoughts and emotions pull us away from the here and now. In our daily lives, we become angry or filled with wanting, and we wonder how emotions still snare us after all these years as Buddhist practitioners. We may even become resistant to sitting and looking at mind, fearing its unwieldiness.

This is where never giving up comes in. If we persist, we will reach the point of relaxing enough to see that mind's occurrences can actually enhance our practice. This doesn't happen in a month or a year, however, so when we begin to wonder, "Why do I do this stuff, this Dharma?" our frustration should alert us to the need for perseverance. Insight often lies just beyond our resistance, and if we persist a little longer, it happens. We should never give in to thoughts about our inadequacies: they are the stepping stones to future adequacies.

We live in an age of instant gratification. My word processor is a miracle that moves sentences around and corrects my spelling. If I need a reference or a phrase, I can consult the Internet, the world's information bank, in an instant. We can call anyone, almost anywhere, on our cell phones. So much is now at our fingertips, we have become spoiled.

The Dharma is not instantly gratifying. We can't just punch up enlightenment. I have wondered if people in the future will be brought to enlightenment with a pill or a tweak of their DNA. It hasn't happened yet, and until it does, persistence is required.

It may seem strange that one should never give up on a discipline that encourages giving up. The Dharma has a lot of conflicting concepts like that; in fact, some people use them to appear steeped in it. They may say, "If you want to get enlightened, it will never happen, because only when you stop wanting will you attain it." Ah, so profound. This is not my intent. What I mean to say is that we should never give up until we do. We should pour our heart into attaining enlightenment until we see that, in truth, it can't be done willfully. That may seem unsatisfying logically—perhaps appropriately so, since what we're attempting is not logical. The resolution lies in sincerity, in pure-heartedness. If we approach the path with trust in the teacher, teachings, and practices, if we do our best, the Dharma will happen. The approach is like riding a train. We don't have to worry whether the train will reach its destination; we trust that it will. The important thing is that we stay on it until it does.

NATURE

A striking aspect of nature is its unbiased
quality, its lack of any agenda.

I just returned from a short trip to the mountains of Colorado. As always, the wonders of nature dazzled me: snow on mountain peaks, towering evergreens, and the brilliant play of light on it all. Along with its beauty, I also enjoyed nature's ever-present spiritual messages. Before turning to them, though, I would first like to discuss the meaning of the term "spiritual" from a Buddhist perspective.

In many religions, "spiritual" indicates a connection with God and the practices surrounding the divine. In Buddhism, however, "spirituality" indicates a connection to Buddha's discoveries about the true nature of mind. Buddha was a great scientist who took nothing for granted. He did not have electron microscopes or knowledge of neurotransmitters, but he did have the observational powers of mind, and he applied those powers to mind itself. The result of his research is known as spirituality.

What does the natural world reveal about Buddhist spirituality? A striking aspect of nature is its unbiased quality, its lack of any agenda. Nature is simply there, without being for or against anything. We can swim in a river or drown in it, and we can delight in the vastness of a great forest or lose our way and perish in it. It makes no difference to nature. Mind shares this fundamental neutrality. When seen uncluttered by concept, mind is also unbiased and simply there; only when afflicted by belief in ego does it depart from this neutral state into discrimination. When we look at a forest or an ocean properly, we are actually observing the true nature of what observes it.

We live a sanitized life in our modern world, one that separates us from the realities our ancestors knew. We eat meat, but we never see animals killed to provide it. People around us are dying all the time—but in hospitals or nursing homes, not in our close-knit village, where we might see them take their last breaths. Death comes to us as a surprise, or even as a mistake of some kind, especially when our young die. We feel death is unacceptable, and we question whether the doctors or nurses failed to apply the technologies correctly. We have forgotten life's ruthlessness.

Nature reminds us of it. Animals constantly kill each other to survive in nature, and death is always present. No moral principles or doctrines guide the natural world—and that is fundamentally true of our lives as well. It is only our concepts about life that make it seem otherwise.

I was once lost in a wilderness area with my son, then in his early teens. At times, I considered that we might not make it out alive. I would not wish the experience on others, but it taught me a lot. Although I had been a Buddhist for some time, the stress of the experience revealed to me how easily we can create and supplicate an all-powerful entity in our time of need, and why it is said there are "no atheists in foxholes." Even in our protected everyday lives, it takes courage to accept what nature and Buddhism are telling us: no one is assisting us in this life. We are fundamentally alone.

Nature shows us that we are alone, and its lack of bias mirrors the nature of our own mind. It also shows us life's fundamental coldness: as the old saying goes, we are not going to get out of this life alive. Humans have made many philosophical attempts to leaven the remorselessness of nature, but it hasn't worked. Although the truth nature shows us is not entirely pleasant, it is the truth. Along with beauty, that truth is its most important aspect.

OTHER

Whenever other arises, problems arise.

Very few people know that "other" is a fallacy. Realized people, however, have no sense of a central entity or ego, and so no sense of separation between themselves and what is putatively outside. As a result, they are other, and other is them.

I once attended a talk Chögyam Trungpa gave to a mostly Christian crowd in Boulder, Colorado. The theme of the talk was "babysitters." He said that we have two babysitters: one that lives at a distance, and another that lives quite close. The distant one was God, and the nearby one was ego. Since this was not a Buddhist crowd, I listened with some trepidation to his comments about God, but he pacified the audience by drinking a whole glass of sake at the end of his talk, diverting their attention from his comments to the well-known issue of his drinking. I find the talk he gave helpful in discussing other, for the concept of "other" is not limited to just conventional sense objects, but to self and God as well.

The world is a frightening place. We no longer worry about saber-toothed tigers, but we may fear losing our spouse or our job. This anxiety causes us to look outside ourselves for assistance. We feel unequipped to deal with the vagaries of life (and with good reason), so we create powerful entities such as God to assist us. Voltaire once said, "If there were no God, it would have been necessary to invent him." That is exactly what happened: there is no God, and humans did create him or her. I know this to be true, because I know that I *am* other. Everything in the world is what I am, so I understand that nothing exists separately from me, including a God who rules the world and determines whether I have sinned or not. Some people may say that God is the same as my experience of undifferentiated mind. If so, more power to them—it doesn't really matter what you call it.

We also treat self as other, even though it seems very close to us. (Or more than close: it is who we are, and we can't conceive of it being otherwise.) Until we accomplish the task of realizing we are nothing, we will not be able to appreciate self's separateness; nevertheless, self is other, and we turn our lives over to it just as some do to God. Self is our live-in babysitter. It tells us what is best for us, what to do, and how to think. We never make a move without checking in with our nanny, self, to see if it's in her best interest. As a result, we never grow up and learn to make our own decisions: we continue to function from the reference point of "me," rather than from the greater awareness and freedom of selflessness.

Whenever other arises, problems arise. The moment we perceive other, we transform emptiness into self, and an interaction begins that invariably leads to self wanting, rejecting, or ignoring other. When we create other, we create emotions that have caused humanity immeasurable pain for a very long time. When we create other, we create hell.

It takes courage to pursue a system that erases other. We might lose our babysitters; if we do, we will have to grow up and face life alone. We have no alternative, however, if we want to understand the true nature of reality and the freedom it represents.

CONFUSION

Our primitive beliefs about reality—
our feelings that we have an ego or self—
greatly complicate our quest for enlightenment.

Happy New Year from the year 2009. Some people arise on New Year's Day confused due to the alcohol they drank the night before. Maybe it's the aging process, but starting off the New Year with a hangover no longer appeals to me. Why begin a new chapter in one's life with a foggy mind? As an acknowledgment of the many people who may be asking themselves the same question, this section is about confusion.

In conventional usage, "confusion" denotes ignorance of where one is, what one is doing, or what is occurring in the environment. We may become confused while driving and head in the wrong direction, or we may become confused in conversation and misunderstand a statement. Or we may simply be confused—not about a topic, but fundamentally—

because of a drug or mental problem. From the standpoint of Buddhism, however, confusion refers to only one thing: whatever excludes mind from enlightenment.

Buddhism describes two fundamental confusions, called the two veils: conflicting emotions and primitive beliefs about reality.

The first veil, conflicting emotions, is the lesser of the two, because we can observe and work with it more easily than the second. Although conflicting emotions are driven by karma (the roots of which lie hidden to our awareness), we can see them occur in our minds. Furthermore, through meditation we can observe that they only become problems when we attach to them.

The second veil resists attempts to observe it. It lies so far beyond our ken that few of us are even aware of it. Our fundamental primitive belief about reality is our confusion about self or ego, the central entity we believe runs our life.

By the way, I have always loved the term "primitive beliefs about reality." Chögyam Trungpa, whom I have mentioned elsewhere, was raised in a culture that lacked the internal combustion engine, electricity, and even the wheel. He was a man of great insight and virtue, but despite his greatness he was considered in the West to be a product of a "backwards" or "primitive" culture. However, his culture was leaps and bounds ahead of the West in understanding reality. From its standpoint, *we* were primitives who held primitive beliefs about reality. Like beauty, primitiveness is in the eye of the beholder.

Our primitive beliefs about reality—our feelings that we have an ego or self—greatly complicate our quest for enlightenment. Being selfless seems counterintuitive to us because we *feel* our self: we feel it think, move our bodies, even do our breathing during meditation. We find it difficult to doubt.

A friend of mine once attended a medical meeting where a young physician presented a new approach to gallbladder surgery. After the presentation, a distinguished older physician objected that he had been doing gallbladder surgeries the traditional way all his life and never had a problem. The younger physician responded that the older surgeon may have been successful with the old procedure, but he had nevertheless done them all wrong. This is also true of life with ego: we may feel we have been getting by just fine, but in truth we have been doing everything wrong.

It can take a long time to realize that ego is our own creation and not truly real: we must remove successive layers of confusion until we are left with the nothing we really are. Since at the outset it is easier to observe how our thoughts and emotions manipulate us, it is usually easier to begin with them and then work down to our primitive beliefs about reality. However, there is always the chance that one penetrating look could reveal the truth of nonego. We can, in an instant, see that we have been fooled all along; but that instant usually results from a mind well prepared by teachings, teacher, and practices.

The first step in overcoming the two veils is understanding that there are such things. At first, we will have to take someone's word for it, but if we persist on the path, we will eventually experience the truth firsthand. When that happens, every day will be new and free of hangovers.

FAITH

To simply read, hear, and have faith in what
the Buddha experienced is not enough.

For some reason, the Christian principles of faith, hope, and
charity came to mind, prompting this entry about faith.

Faith is a much-desired quality in many religions. The
greater one's faith becomes, the more devout one is perceived to be. Discussing religion with "people of faith," one
encounters faith as quickly as the title suggests. For example,
when devout Christians are asked a spiritual question, they
will often refer the questioner to the teachings of the Bible,
in whose divine origins they have faith—even though the
questioner may not share their assurance.

Faith also plays a role in Buddhism. At the outset, all Buddhists lack realization, and enter the path with faith that the
teachings, teachers, and practices will help them attain it. But
to base Buddhism on faith alone runs counter to the whole
idea of it, because Buddhism is about actually experiencing

enlightenment. To simply read, hear, and have faith in what the Buddha experienced is not enough. Buddhism is not a faith-based discipline but an experience-based one: faith is only needed until one actually encounters what one has faith in.

For this reason, I have serious problems with spiritual endeavors that depend exclusively on faith. If one has faith that God exists, that faith should eventually be confirmed by meeting God in the flesh (or whatever he comes in). To sustain oneself on faith alone, without it eventually leading to an actual experience, doesn't make sense to me. How many people would spend their lives fishing in a lake without catching a fish, because they had faith that someday they would? Or who would take up fishing at all, if the sport decreed that having faith in fish was more important than actually catching them?

For my part, I suspect that relying on faith is often the doctrine of those who can't actually produce what their faith is based on. Of course, believers always have proof that the supernatural does come to them, that it does help them and grants their wishes. But they never consider that the relief they feel could simply be a creation of their own minds. Faith can do that to people.

Enlightenment, the fruition of Buddhism, can be experienced. It is real; indeed it is the most real of human experiences. The true nature of mind is not religious legerdemain; for the past 2,500 years, countless practitioners have experienced realization, and many have documented it. The Dharma concerns what is real, and faith sustains its practitioners only until that reality is experienced. After that, faith is no longer needed.

Hope

Two major problems arise when
we turn to the future with hope.

I took the time to look up the history of faith, hope, and charity in Christian thought, and found that some of the great Church fathers such as St. Thomas and St. Augustine wrote about them. As with much Church doctrine, however, I couldn't understand exactly what they intended to say, although it was clear that faith, hope, and charity are principles of Christianity.

When I find dense, circuitous explanations of spiritual principles in the Christian or any other spiritual tradition, I become suspicious. Why should the truth be complicated? Of course, terms in Buddhism such as "nonduality" and "emptiness" can be difficult to understand—not because their presentation is complex, but because one must experience them to appreciate what they mean.

Hope, I'm afraid, comes off even worse than faith in Buddhism: some faith is applicable to the Dharma, but not hope. In fact, a major sign that one has accomplished the Buddhist path is that hope and fear desist. Buddhism couples hope with fear, because hope is the counterpart of fear: if one exists, so does the other. In confusion, we are always shuttling between these two extremes. If something goes wrong with our car or our health, we hope it won't be bad and fear that it will. This painful alternation between hope and fear creates agitated mental activity that obscures the true nature of mind. As a result, hope and fear are viewed as obstacles that must be overcome.

Hope is problematic because it is directed to the future, a realm of little use to Buddhists. Importantly, although there is a path in Buddhism, it goes nowhere. Chögyam Trungpa wrote a book whose title, *The Path is the Goal,* makes this point. Although we progress through stages of Buddhism, each stage can only happen right now, right before our eyes. What is happening right now in our life is our path, and the better we attend to it, the faster we progress on it. The path is not simply a means to reach the goal; the path itself is the goal. One can see how poorly hope fits with this approach to life.

Two major problems arise when we turn to the future with hope. First, the future does not exist. All that has ever been is now, so turning our attention to the future removes us from the only reality there is. Second, the future often fails to turn out as we expect. As a result, we spend a lot of time hoping for things that lose their relevance when the "future" arrives. For example, we may hope to enjoy a pleasant retirement and expend a lot of effort acquiring the means to do so, only to die before we reach it. We entertained hopes of and took steps toward something that never materialized. Of course, planning ahead does have its merits, but we should understand that all our plans, even those far into the future, can only be made in the present.

A cousin of hope, one closer to the Buddhist approach to the future, is aspiration. In Vajrayana Buddhism, aspiration is employed as a means to attain the qualities of one's teacher or guru—an important part of the process that leads to enlightenment. Aspiration is a yearning or longing for these qualities, and as such it focuses on what may happen in the future. However, properly trained practitioners understand that like anything in life, aspiration can only be actualized in the present. And unlike hope, aspiration involves much more commitment and strength of purpose than simply fantasizing that someday something will fall into our lap.

I recognize that hope is a very powerful force in mind, and I am not treating it lightly. Although I understand its problems from a Buddhist standpoint, as a physician I never take it away from my patients. Only very few patients—and I have known some—have the courage to live or die without hope. In my own life, there have been times when only hope seemed to sustain me, so I'm not being cavalier about its importance. On the other hand, if we wish to know the truth of the Dharma, at some point we will have to transcend hope.

CHARITY

───────

*We might ask how the West perverted such an
honorable goal as charity with greed and criminality.*

───────

I consulted a dictionary about "charity," and found that it is,
first, man's love for God—which is above all other love—as
well as the love for his fellow man that results from that
love; and, second, caring for the poor and downtrodden.
I presume that Christians refer to both definitions when
they speak about charity, but the second is the one I wish
to discuss.

I have problems with charity, particularly the kind represented by charitable organizations, because I have experienced the ironies of those organizations at their worst. I
have been extorted by charities in the workplace, forced
to give not from a desire to help others, but from fear of
the peer pressure I would encounter if I didn't help fill up
their "fund-thermometers." I have seen heads of charities

use charity money for personal gain: I remember when the most successful CEO in the history of United Way was jailed for stealing large amounts of its funds. For many years I witnessed a famous entertainer use the mannerisms of people stricken with a neurological problem to get laughs and make money; he then started a charity for those same victims, which brought him further fame and fortune.

On a larger scale, Christian nations have taken many viable cultures, such as those present in the Americas before their colonization by Europe, and systematically destroyed them with disease and violence. They have then prided themselves on supporting those very cultures they had reduced to penury with charity. This offends my own idea of compassion, which is well articulated in a tried-and-true medical saying: "First, do no harm." I have seen rulers around the world, the recipients of American international largesse, steal money meant for their people to buy tanks and helicopters in support of the activities that had caused their nations' poverty in the first place. One country built a nuclear arsenal with American munificence, even though it was stipulated that the money could not be used to build nuclear weapons.

I have also seen charity turned against Buddhism. Buddhists are sometimes portrayed as selfish, spending their lives sitting in meditation trying to attain personal salvation without any concern for others' needs. These accusations stem from an ignorance of Buddhism and life in general. We might ask in response how the West perverted such an honorable goal as charity with greed and criminality. What happened? One thing that happened was that the West never sat in meditation and observed how mind operates. It never understood that unless mind settles into peace and loving-kindness, the charity it proposes will be perverted, or that ego corrupts all attempts to benefit others with its concern for benefiting itself.

I remember Chögyam Trungpa discussing his time as a refugee in India after the Chinese takeover of Tibet. He spoke of receiving, I believe, powdered milk from a Christian organization. The milk containers had Christian promotions printed on them. My teacher had witnessed the destruction of his culture; at that point, all he had was the Dharma. He didn't need to be bludgeoned by Christian attempts at truth in order to receive his milk, and he didn't need to feel that Buddhism was for those who needed charity and Christianity for those who provided it. He could face death from starvation without a murmur—but not the undermining of Dharma, the basis of his culture and himself. This is the sort of thing that people who haven't sat in meditation do to others without realizing it.

The Buddhist path includes a stage called the Mahayana. Those who believe Buddhism to be without concern for others should familiarize themselves with it. Entering the Mahayana, one takes an oath to forswear enlightenment until all other sentient beings attain it, a great charitable act. Mahayana practitioners, called bodhisattvas, dedicate their lives to helping others attain enlightenment—not by putting messages on milk cans, but by committing their lives to them. An example is Chögyam Trungpa, who died at age forty-eight after giving his last drop of energy to others. People with questions about the currency of compassion in Buddhism should familiarize themselves with the Mahayana and the bodhisattvas who practice it.

As the old saying goes, charity begins at home. In Buddhism, however, our real home is something more personal than the hearth: it is our self, and the greatest charity we can extend to it is to discover that it doesn't exist. When we accomplish that, we will naturally turn our attention toward others in the form of selfless charity.

How Does One Know?

Realization is an experience without an experiencer.

Realization is the experience of the true nature of mind, empty/awareness. So how does one know when one encounters it? This may seem a silly question, but many years in the world have shown me differently.

Fortunately, realization has a number of unique qualities that distinguish it from other experiences. One is that it changes the world's appearance forever: all phenomena become illusory, dreamlike, and vivid. Pies, pistols, and peach trees lose their realness, and never return to their previous state. Chögyam Trungpa described this experience in a *sadhana* (spiritual practice) called the Sadhana of Mahamudra: "Whatever is seen with the eyes is vividly unreal in emptiness, yet there is still form." In those few words, he describes how the world changes in realization, while making the further point that form remains, undercutting the misconception that realization is nihilistic.

Another sign of realization is that no one or thing experiences or creates it. Realization is an experience without an experiencer. This quality of egolessness is a good test not only for realization but for any experience on the path. A saying from the eleventh-century teacher Atisha states: "All dharmas agree at one point." The "point" where all dharma teachings meet is egolessness. Everything we do is weighed by how much it reduces our sense of and allegiance to self, and we can judge any progress we make in Buddhism by how much of our ego remains in that "progress." How much of what we think we have accomplished is still in the service of an ego we have yet to fully see through?

Another quality of realization is that it does not differ among people. The realization of Gautama Buddha remains the same for all enlightened people since. Reading the insights of realized teachers who lived 2,500 years ago is as easy as reading the morning newspaper for those who share their experience. For this reason, another test of realization is how well one can understand the writings of acknowledged teachers of the past, and, more importantly, how well they agree with one's experience of self and the world.

Finally, the experience of realization brings a sense of rest and freedom beyond compare. Its restfulness is fundamental, beyond the duality of activity and rest, and its freedom is not contrasted to any type of confinement, but is a complete, limitless, unconditional freedom.

To gain the insight of realization requires a lot of time and effort. The process generally starts with understanding the absence of ego or self. Next, one progresses to the experience of the true nature of phenomena. In my case, this progression took fifteen years—fifteen years in which I found a buddha for a teacher and energetically committed myself to practice and learning. The remaining insights, nonduality and empty/awareness, also require years of daily practice and solitary retreats. I mention this to provide some sense of the real commitment and time required to attain realization. I have met people who never practiced or studied Buddhism, who believed that after a psychic hiccup they had awakened to the truth. It doesn't happen that way, and such a belief misleads others and stops one's own progress on the path.

I have outlined some of realization's characteristics. If what I have described is your experience, you are realized. Congratulations. I'm sorry there is no one to accept the accolade.

As for determining if others are realized, I might recommend a little test: ask them to describe how objects appear to them. If without hesitation they report the world as I described above, with the same assurance as if relating the color of their own eyes, they could have it—or, more to the point, be it.

TRUTH

The truth suffers both from those who
don't believe in it and those who do.

Truth has become suspect. No longer do we speak of *the* truth, but of "my" or "your" truth: parsed by philosophers, theologians, social scientists, and the law, truth no longer signifies one thing but many. It is outdated in the postmodern world, having become just another tool in support of each person's viewpoint.

Fewer and fewer people believe in the truth; and conversely, many believe they have it, further diluting it. All faiths lay claim to the truth, and most are willing to fight for it. In fact, even practitioners of the same religion will fight amongst themselves. The truth suffers both from those who don't believe in it and those who do.

In Buddhism, there are two truths. The first is relative truth, the conventional truth brought to us by our senses.

Relative truth appears to be the true nature of things, but it is flawed by duality—by the implication that experience involves an interaction between something experienced and someone experiencing it. The second truth is absolute truth: the real truth, a nonnegotiable truth that has always been and always will be. Absolute truth is the true nature of mind. It shows us that what sees and what is seen are the same.

The two truths are nicely illustrated by *The Matrix,* a movie whose plot involves machines plugging dreams into the minds of humans while using their bodies for heat and electricity. We can compare relative truth to the dream world of the "plugged-in." To them, that world is valid: they suffer if they break its laws, and feel happiness if they follow them. But Neo, the hero, becomes unplugged and realizes that he has been living in a dream. Like a truly realized person in our world, he knows both absolute and relative truth—the machines' world, and the world he sees when unplugged. He sees that relative truth seems real and has consequences, but he also sees that it is flawed and not true reality. Moreover, his insight gives him extraordinary powers in the dream world, much as Buddhist mahasiddhas (highly magical, enlightened beings) wield in our world.

At the highest levels of understanding, absolute and relative truth coexist. We can take death as an example: although we experience it as a profound change in our conventional existence, it has little impact on absolute reality. Chögyam Trungpa once said, "When you die, space does not blink," meaning that the absolute truth of emptiness is not affected by the relative truth of death. Even during the most profound change in our conventional experience, absolute experience remains unmoved. Even in death, the most radical of human events, the two truths function together.

I find it quite wonderful that there is absolute truth. Like most people, I live in a world dominated by relative truth, so I am encouraged to know there really is a pole star around which all human activity revolves. Simply experiencing the wonder of absolute truth is not enough, though: we must also help those struggling in relative truth to find it and incorporate it into their lives.

Two Minds

---

*Since the occurrences of regular mind and
what they occur in are both empty, they
are inseparable in their shared emptiness.*

When we say we are "of two minds," we usually mean we are unable to choose between two different perspectives on a subject. In truth, although few of us realize it, we are always of two minds—not because we are indecisive, but because we actually have two different minds.

Mental activities comprise the mind we are more familiar with. This mind makes decisions, such as whether to buy a car and what to cook for dinner. It is also our emotions, worrying about our children or a new spot that appeared on our arm. Although this mind runs our life, and although we constantly follow its directions, we seldom pay attention to it until something unwelcome occurs and it begins to bother us. Then we might say we are "losing our mind"; but we aren't really losing it, we're just noticing we can't control it. This is the first mind.

The second mind is the mind of realization, the environment in which the first mind occurs. A Zen analogy likens it to a body of water, and the first mind's activities to a sword slashing through the water, which disappear in the same instant they are made. The stuff of realized mind, though, is not water but nothingness, a limitless space without form, color, or dimensions.

So we have the mind of our thoughts and emotions, and the mind in which they occur. These two minds are really one, but since we are all born confused, we generally only experience the first mind and not the second. When we first experience the mind of realization, we find that it has the same quality of nothingness or emptiness as its activities. Since the occurrences of regular mind and what they occur in are both empty, they are inseparable in their shared emptiness. For this reason, each thought or emotion we have has the potential to bring us to realization: it can show us that its emptiness is the same as that of the mind it occurs in.

This is not religious dogma, but a description of what we can actually experience. With time and effort, each of us can experience the two minds, and see them to be one. We do this through meditation: by sitting and observing mind, we can recognize and become familiar with its activities, and over time we can quiet and slow them until they change from a rushing stream into a quiet lake. This gives us the opportunity to experience mind's nature. When we see the lake, undisturbed by the turbulence of the running stream, we realize that it is composed of clear, still water. If the lake turns back into a stream later, we are not fooled: we now know it to be made of water, and not a white material we can't identify. This is how we come to see the two minds as one.

After we develop some experience of the two minds, we may be surprised that mental and emotional upheaval continues to roil mind and obscure its nature. Even if we know the world is unreal, it still influences us, like a riveting movie. I remember seeing the movie *Alien*, and finding it so frightening I almost walked out. I knew the movie was just projected images on a screen, but that didn't help. I was still scared. We become especially prone to being mesmerized by the world, and deprived of the experience of the two minds as one, if we fail to maintain a meditation practice; but even that is not foolproof. There was a Buddhist practice center near where I live called Rocky Mountain Dharma Center. (The name has since been changed.) One wag I know used to call it Rocky Mountain Drama Center, and the designation was accurate. Even though it was a practice center, a lot more than realized mind went on there.

The best way to approach the two minds is to see them as one. Seeing their union in emptiness, we can use the occurrences of regular mind to connect us with the freedom of realized mind. When that happens, our hopes and fears will no longer confine us but free us.

SPEED KILLS

A mind out of control can be as
dangerous as a vehicle out of control.

Speed kills. I have known this for a long time—certainly since my time as a young physician with the Marines in the Vietnam War, when I saw what an M16 rifle round can do to the human skull.

The M16 was the standard-issue rifle for most Marines in Vietnam, and for me as well. (I was not a Marine but a Navy physician; the Marines do not have physicians.) It shot a .223 round, a small piece of lead, at very high velocity. In physics, $E_k=mv^2$: the energy an object imparts in a collision is equal to its mass times the square of its velocity. This means that a bullet doesn't have to be very big to do a lot of damage if it travels at high enough speed.

One night, I was called to see a dead Marine who had moved on a night ambush and been shot by his own men.

I couldn't understand how he died until I felt his skull: it had the consistency of a wet paper bag. A round had hit his head at great speed, shattering every bone in his skull and destroying his brain. When I felt that Marine's head, I really understood that speed kills.

Speed is dangerous not only with regard to the tangible, but the intangible as well. Strong emotions such as anger cause mind to speed up, and this acceleration causes us to say and do regrettable things—they simply happen before we realize it. For example, most homicides are between acquaintances. As two friends drink in a bar, their minds gather momentum over some trivial issue, and one kills the other. A mind out of control is as dangerous as a vehicle out of control: if we grab on to the energy of anger or desire, it can take us for a high-speed ride in which everything, even the preciousness of life, becomes blurred. That's why in Buddhism we learn to work with mind's speed.

Recently, I vacationed in Panama, and I think it's the most beautiful place I have ever been. The variety of trees and plants and diversity of animals and bird life is glorious. The same cannot be said for the lives of some of its human inhabitants. I walked past one Panama City *barrio*—something I don't recommend—whose smell reminded me of a pig farm.

One day I passed a barrio in a cab. The driver (a nice person, as are Panamanians in general) was manfully working with what passes for my Spanish when, stopping at a light, we saw an arresting sight. A lady in her early thirties, whom it was still possible to see had been beautiful, stood in the street searching for enough change to take the cab in front of us. She was barefoot, dressed in filthy shorts and a blouse, and, to a physician, obviously hooked on "speed," the street term for amphetamine. She was dying of a drug that accelerated her metabolism to unlivable levels. I summoned the only word I could think of for "speed" in Spanish, *rápido,* incorrectly using an adjective instead of a noun. The cab driver answered slowly, repeating in my fractured Spanish so I could understand, *"Rápido, se muerte, rápido."* Fast dies fast.

The woman's situation may seem exceptional to us, but many of us suffer from a mind that is also pushing us to speeds we can't safely maintain. As a physician, I see this every day with my patients, recorded in their high blood pressures, strokes, heart attacks, and mental illnesses. The speed of mind is killing them.

Buddhism has no desire to speed anywhere, whether to altered mental states or connections with the cosmic. Here suits Buddhism fine. Instead of speeding things up, it employs meditation to slow thoughts and emotions down, so we can see them for what they are: simply occurrences of mind without any special credentials. It teaches us a natural way to prevent mind from reaching speeds that kill.

HOME

There is only one exception to the rule that we can never
go home again, and that is the mind of realization.

Some years ago, a book was written called *You Can't Go Home Again*. I never read it, but I found the title haunting and true. The following story about Milarepa, the great eleventh-century Tibetan yogin, proves the point.

After having studied for some time with his teacher Marpa, Milarepa felt a longing to visit his home. He received permission from Marpa to leave, and returned to find his birthplace quite unlike what he remembered: his mother had died, his home and fields were in ruins, and his sister was reduced to begging. Milarepa was overcome by grief at what he saw, and at the knowledge that his home was gone forever. Returning to our homes, if we still have them, may be less dramatic than it was for Milarepa; nevertheless, his experience holds true for us as well.

I think of my son, who has been out of our home for five years, first in college and then working. Recently, he came home, and it was like the old days. His mother and I smiled as he returned to his old habits of playing the piano, sleeping in, and staying up with friends or video games. It was a bit trying at times, but we didn't say anything: ours is his home, the only place where he can really relax. I know that inevitably and sadly all this too will change, that the time will come when we are dead, the house is sold, and all is but a memory.

There is only one exception to the rule that we can never go home again, and that is the mind of realization. This mind is the only permanent home we will ever find, the only place to which we can return and discover all we treasure unchanged. Being timeless, it never ages; being without substance, it never disintegrates. Even our death does not affect the mind of realization, because it never belonged to us: it inhabits our body while we live, and merges with the nothingness it always was when we die.

Writing of home reminds me of a problem I see as a physician. Occasionally, I admit an older patient to the hospital who becomes confused at night, calling out or wandering the halls. (I had one patient who used to wander into other patients' rooms at night and take their things. He wasn't a thief, just confused, a distinction that made little difference to the other patients.) The patient's spouse or caregiver assures me that he or she is never confused at home, and testing for neurologic or metabolic problems usually yields nothing abnormal. Experience alerts me that the problem is "sundowning," a transient confusion brought on by the loss of familiar reference points in a strange room at night. The objects and schedules of home help orient people's minds to the here and now, and being removed from them causes these patients to become disoriented and lose touch with the environment. They suffer the loss of two homes: their physical one, and consequently their mental one. Homes are important. We derive solace and sanity from them. Whether physical, mental, or both, losing them disorients us and discovering them helps us return to reality. It is therefore one of the Dharma's great gifts to provide us with a permanent home in mind.

Realization is our only chance to go home again. It alone fulfills our longing for a loving, restful place that will always be ours. My son will learn that all material homes crumble, and that inevitably his too will be gone. I hope by then he has found a home in mind.

Space

"Space" is a helpful word in the Dharma. Although
it fails in a number of ways to describe the real feeling
of realized mind, it provides a useful conceptual
framework for its no-thingness or emptiness.

Mind is often said to resemble space, and it does. Like the
space between the stars and planets, it is boundless, inde-
scribable in terms of color or form, insubstantial, all-perva-
sive, and without the characteristics of a thing.

Having drawn the analogy, though, we must recognize
the important differences between space and mind. Unlike
"outer" space, the space of mind is both outside and inside
us, since with its discovery the notions of outside and inside
dissolve. Also unlike space, mind possesses awareness, which
allows it to hear, see, taste, smell, and feel. Finally, mind feels
rich, filled with a sense of "suchness" or heaviness of being.
(A movie was once made about the lightness of being;

someday someone should make one about its heaviness.) Although the true experience of mind is not laden with meaning, since in its natural state awareness does not assign a sense of particular importance or unimportance to anything, "meaning" is as close as one might come to describing its heft.

The space of mind is commonly called emptiness. Emptiness is nothingness—"no-thingness"—or space with the qualities I have described. We and the world are pervaded by this emptiness. In medicine, when we look at tissues under a microscope, we see the structures that define them as liver or lung tissue, but we always see something else in the background: the environment the structures live in, called ground substance. Emptiness is the ground substance of reality. When we look at trees or thimbles with the mind of realization, their forms appear in emptiness, giving them an airy, light, illusory quality. When we look inside ourselves (so to speak), we also see emptiness—or, more precisely, feel it.

I love certain words, among them "emptiness": it gets directly to the point about the nature of mind and reality. I sometimes wonder whether I could have found the precise word to describe the space of realization. Being unable to share one's experiences with others is painful enough without lacking the words to describe them. We all owe a lot to those who find accurate descriptions of reality.

"Space" is a helpful word in the Dharma. Although it fails in a number of ways to describe the real feeling of realized mind, it provides a useful conceptual framework for its no-thingness or emptiness. This framework can help us, as long as we don't mistake it for mind itself.

No Medals

If we expect that realization will bring us committed students, or even that others will recognize our attainment, we will be disappointed.

Chögyam Trungpa once said that no one receives a medal for being the greatest bodhisattva. In a more up-to-date expression of the same idea, his Dharma heir, the Vajra Regent, said that "no grants are given for enlightenment."

Before experiencing realization, we might expect that the insights we gain will be readily recognized and appreciated. I had the good fortune of quickly experiencing the enlightened nature of my teacher's mind and the magic surrounding it, and I believed that if and when I succeeded on the path I too would gain that magic. It hasn't happened yet. And though I am thankfully able to write about it, what happened to me still remains largely unrecognized in the day-to-day world.

There are no medals for realization—I am serving notice to anyone who has experienced it. If we expect that realization will bring us committed students, or even that others will recognize our attainment, we will be disappointed. There is a saying in Zen: "You're enlightened—now get a job."

With time, I have come to understand that wanting recognition for realization is actually missing the point, because it is sufficient unto itself. To completely experience it is to require nothing else. At first, before understanding this, I hoped that others would acknowledge my achievement. I would look into their eyes, expecting they would experience what I had experienced looking into my teacher's. Nothing happened. I bought glasses that didn't reflect on the surface, so others could see my eyes better. Nothing happened. I taught groups of senior students and debated recognized teachers in front of many others. Nothing happened. No one became realized looking into my eyes or hearing what I said, or showed any indication of knowing what I represented. I felt like Rodney Dangerfield.

When I first "settled the great matter," as they say in the old Zen texts, I became upset if people doubted my understanding, since it is a grave error in the Dharma to proclaim attainment one doesn't have. I was angered by the implication that I would not only lie, but transgress such an important law. Over time, though, I stopped caring. We are always giving up on the path, and I gave up wanting others to believe me.

Then, as insight matured and I found living in it was all the fulfillment needed, the desire to be recognized faded.

Realization is the pinnacle of human achievement, but until we fully achieve it, even it has a downside. Implicit in it is the desire to share it with others, but that may not be possible. Having become rich and generous, we walk down the street handing out thousand-dollar bills, but no one wants them. We may want to shake people and say, "Take this—it's a real thousand-dollar bill," but our entreaties only make people more wary.

I recognize that my own deficiencies have hindered my spreading my good fortune to others. I am not a buddha like my teacher. I am nowhere near his level of attainment, with his ability to change others' perceptions and adjust the workings of the world at large. This makes it much more difficult for others to appreciate what I represent. Also, and I say this humbly, I was a special student of his: one who quickly understood what he was. In retrospect, I understand that I had a strong natural affinity for authentic teachers, both in my need for realization and in my ability to recognize the Dharma in others. It is presumptuous to expect others to be the same way.

In summary, if you are realized, please accept my congratulations. Appreciate and take pleasure in your attainment, whether or not you are successful in sharing it with others. And don't expect any medals.

OPENING

When we let go, we are left with nothing;
when we open, we are left with everything,
and that everything rubs on our exposed organs.

Earlier, I mentioned seeing a teacher unclench his fist as a visual demonstration of letting go in the Dharma. The same gesture could also be used to demonstrate the process of opening.

We could say that letting go and opening are much the same, since opening is really letting go of protecting ourselves. In reality, however, the two experiences feel quite different. Letting go involves giving something up; opening involves exposing oneself, like exposing the palm inside one's fist. When we let go, something leaves us; but when we open, it feels like someone grabbed our chest and split it open, exposing our heart and lungs to the outside. When we let go, we are left with nothing; when we open, we are left with everything, and that everything rubs on our exposed organs.

Opening can be quite helpful. If we open to the thoughts that hassle us during meditation rather than fighting them, we find they interfere less with our practice. Accepting them allows us to relax, which is an important aspect of meditation. Similarly, when we open to our experience instead of grasping or rejecting it, we see more clearly how manipulating it has blinded us to its real nature.

When I first really opened, I was surprised at how closed-off I had been. I had been congratulated for openness through the years, and believed it was a strong point of mine. Then the Dharma proved me wrong: I saw how my fears of being found wanting as a man, physician, gentleman, provider, father, husband, and member of society had kept me from really opening. I found, as well, how much the fear of death influenced me. When I opened, I understood how these things weighed on my chest, and how badly I needed to remove them.

The importance of opening is well demonstrated in the famous statement by Lao Tzu: "The perfect Dao is without difficulty, save that it avoids picking and choosing." The essence of opening is unconditional acceptance, learning to accept life as it happens without picking or choosing. We have to learn to open to the elements, allow the rain to fall inside us, the snow to chill us, the wind to blow through our organs. Only then can we be free, and thereby of benefit to others. If we have unresolved areas, places where we are unable to open, the world will find them and snap us shut like a clamshell.

The Dharma is about freedom, and our progress on the path is toward greater freedom. Bliss is often said to be the fruition of the path, but that bliss arises from freedom. Freedom is the real fruition, one we will never attain unless we open. As long as life's trials make us retreat into ourselves and into evaluations of good and bad, we will never be free.

We all know that opening unconditionally will cause us pain. The world is ruthless: it will pummel us, break our heart, and tear it from our chest. Christ was crucified and Milarepa poisoned—that's what happens to completely open people. Nevertheless, we must carry on. If we allow fear to dominate us, we will lose our openness, and our ability to understand and benefit others. We have to be willing to tolerate the pain of openness to be of benefit to this world.

ENTERTAINMENT

We have to stop and look inside.

Dilgo Khysentse Rinpoche was one of the great Buddhist teachers of the twentieth century, whom I had the good fortune to meet on one of his visits to America in the 1980s. During one visit, an American student, excited by the flourishing of Dharma in the country at that time, expressed to Khysentse Rinpoche his expectation that a lot of enlightened American practitioners would soon appear. Rinpoche said he didn't think so, because in America, "there is too much entertainment."

America is the entertainment capital of the world. If you want entertainment in any shape or form, America is the place to get it. Most Americans never think twice about enjoying it: our hard work entitles us to it, and we need it to take our minds off the stresses of life. How could anyone find fault with it?

What only a few know, however, is that entertainment also takes life. Moment to moment, watching TV or a movie steals our attention, preventing us from appreciating our own existence. Even though *I Love Lucy* may seem an integral part of that existence, and even though our memories of sports and music events may feel like highlights of it, the fact remains that in those pleasantest of times we were being cheated out of our real life.

Entertainment is also somewhat suspicious: why is it so addictive? The answer is that it shelters us from our fear of nothingness—a fear so pervasive that we may not realize just how much we entertain ourselves to escape it. For example, we may not consider that angry, excited, or obsessive thought qualifies as entertainment. It does, though, as does every other diversion we choose out of our terror of discovering we are actually nothing.

As the Buddha said, "life is pain." We all wish to avoid pain, so we try different ways to ignore it. Often, however, we might notice that when the entertainment ends our stress returns. I remember the stress of medical school quite vividly. My roommate and I would often take Saturday night, our one night off a week, to go to a movie. What a relief it was to relax and get caught up in the movie—and how terrible it was to walk out and recall the big tests coming up the next week. I learned in those days that entertainment was only a short-term fix. Only much later did I find the permanent one: relating to my problems through meditation rather than brushing them aside with entertainment.

We have to stop and look inside. When we do, we might find boredom, or our problems. As unpleasant as those discoveries may be, we have to start there and work with them. They are our real life, and if we persist in looking at them, eventually we will discover what lies behind them and how it reconciles them.

No entertainment compares with the restfulness and fulfillment of realization. Admittedly, experiencing realization takes a lot of time and energy, and is never guaranteed. Entertainment is a more certain and quicker approach, but I put my money on realization because it is the only permanent fix. Entertainment pulls us away from the direct experience of mind, the only place where true relief exists.

Entertainment distracts us from our own life, provides only short-term fixes, impedes our chances for realization, and is addictive. If we understand these problems, we can do ourselves a big favor and turn off the TV—or stop our obsessive worrying—and sit down quietly with our existence. Then, we will find the greatest pleasure existence provides: the moment-to-moment experience of itself.

SIMPLICITY

---

*Even when what surrounds the Dharma seems
complicated, the actual experience of it remains simple.*

A lot goes on in Buddhism. We have the teachings, the
practices, and relationships with the teacher and our fellow
students. In some denominations we progress through various practices, each involving introductory programs that
often require travel. (Tibetan Buddhism in particular has
been criticized as having too many practices, with too many
complicated rituals. A Zen adept I know calls them "all the
bells and whistles.") In fact, we can get so lost in the trap-
pings of the Dharma that we miss its main point, attaining
enlightenment.

Even when what surrounds the Dharma seems complicated, its actual experience remains simple. Furthermore,
when that simplicity is realized, complexity also becomes
simple. This is why the founder of Soto Zen, Dogen Zenji,

had his most advanced students cook: he felt they possessed the insight needed to simplify cooking, the most complicated job in the monasteries of his day.

The Dharma is about nothing, and nothing is simple. It has no components; if it did, it wouldn't be nothing. Because it is everywhere, it doesn't move, so it is easy to find. In fact, nothing is so simple that many people find it boring. When I first experienced Chögyam Trungpa's mind and everything stopped in mine, I felt great bliss. Finding that too good to be true, I looked into his eyes to assure myself of his authenticity, and immediately encountered an intense, cloying boredom that I could barely tolerate for a moment. His mind, along with bliss, contained the complete simplicity of nothing—which is not to say he was simple-minded. After all, he founded the first contemplative university in the New World, created an international Buddhist community, and published dozens of books that have sold millions of copies.

The Dharma is also about opening, and opening brings simplicity. When we become closed to the world, we create a lot of complexity for ourselves trying to maintain that closed approach. For example, if we can't open to aging, we may spend a lot of time and energy trying to stay young with face-lifts, Botox injections, or sports cars. Without openness, we also exhaust ourselves feigning emotions: to paraphrase T. S. Eliot's "The Love Song of J. Alfred Prufrock," we must "prepare a face to meet the faces that we meet." Conversely, opening is effortless. Once done, it requires no maintenance. What could be simpler than that?

Simplicity can't be discussed without mentioning ego. Ego complicates our life, because it demands that we align our experiences to confirm it. In fact, ego is the basis of life's complexity: it is the head of our bureaucracy, and everything must be cleared through it and evaluated against its master plans. Because it occupies and limits awareness, it also adds a layer of obscurity and complexity to our perception of the world. Also, it is very insecure—as only nothing amidst nothing can be—so its decisions are subject to change. No wonder our neck and back hurt after a day's work, when we have been dealing with the incompetent bureaucracy of ego.

Part of a sadhana written by Chögyam Trungpa reads, "The siddha enjoys himself with great simplicity," *siddha* being a term for an enlightened being. Many things could be said about such a person, so I find it instructive that simplicity is the attribute my teacher chose. Upon reflection, I believe this is because simplicity is the culmination of so many aspects of the realized state.

CREDENTIALS

---

*Fundamentally, credentials are
an expression of vulnerability.*

In my life, I have managed to acquire more than a few credentials: doctor of medicine, board certification in internal medicine and rheumatology, and other academic, athletic, and spiritual credentials. I like having them, because they grant me respect and access to people and places I wouldn't otherwise have. Nor do I feel sheepish about enjoying what I have earned after countless hours of study and work. (In my training in medicine, for example, I sometimes worked with gravely ill patients every day, and every second night.) I earned my credentials and I enjoy them, especially since I discovered they are not me.

For a very long time I had this wrong, and I paid the price. My efforts to fulfill everything that I and others expected of me as a physician robbed me of much of what I treasure about life. Fortunately, over time, I realized that credentials are exactly what we make them. Making them who we are is a serious mistake, because we are actually nothing. When one day I saw that I was really the hole and not the donut, credentials became much less of a burden.

We make credentials out of much more than our work. Even our name is one. When we are born, we are somewhat randomly given a name. Our mother may tell us that she strongly considered Egbert or Louella before finally choosing Mortimer or Pleance. It was arbitrary. Like all credentials, names have hidden problems. We may be saddled with a name others find amusing, or one people misread or cannot pronounce. My wife's name is Arla, and I can't count the times she has been misidentified as Darla, Marla, or Carla. It is doubly painful to mistake a credential for who we are, and then be teased or mislabeled because of it.

Negative credentials are as potent at supporting ego as positive ones. As a child singing in the school choir, I was told after several songs to "mouth the words," because I was a "monotone." I didn't know exactly what that meant, but I knew it was bad enough for the choirmaster to tell me to stop singing. As a result of that brief comment long ago, I carried the credential for many years that "I" could not sing.

My teacher once said, in his colorful way, that if you met a mahasiddha he would probably piss you off. I believe our adherence to credentials is the reason. A mahasiddha would long since have discarded his or her credentials, and, being completely open and fearless, would quickly tweak one of ours.

Fundamentally, credentials are an expression of vulnerability. Our sense of self is not as secure as we suppose—if it were, we would never notice it. Self sticks out only because it is separate from our being, something we created. Because we feel the awkwardness of ego, we develop credentials to make it more comfortable. We become Doctor, Professor, Judge, or Waste Manager So-and-So.

Our sense of self is as though we'd stuck an elephant's trunk on our nose: no matter how hard we might try, we could never erase the suspicion that it might not belong there. Our credentials are ways of reassuring ourselves that we should have trunks. Someday, if we are lucky, the Dharma will cause our trunks to drop off, and we will no longer need to rationalize them.

THIS AND THAT

---

*Much of our progress in the Dharma is toward
recognizing the nonexistence of This, the
unreality of That, and the inseparability
of the two in their shared emptiness.*

I have always found the counterintuitiveness of the Dharma
encouraging. If Buddha had wanted to stay within humanity's comfort zone, or if his only interest had been to magne-
tize a card-carrying clientele, he would have taught a different type of spirituality. He would have developed something
much more graspable and hopeful—perhaps with a savior
figure and himself as an intermediary to promulgate its
wishes. Buddha had to be telling the truth as he experienced
it to teach things as implausible as the absence of self.

One of the more shocking tenets of the Dharma is its
refutation of This and That. Most people experience reality
as someone inside, This, relating to a world outside, That. In

the Dharma, this construct is seen to be false. In fact, much of our progress in the Dharma is toward recognizing the nonexistence of This, the unreality of That, and the inseparability of the two in their shared emptiness.

Why is it important to see through This and That? As an illustration, let's say we have a small yard where we would like to put our dog and some chickens. We fence the yard into halves, one half for the chickens and the other for the dog; but after doing so, we find that the yard is now too small for the dog. This is like when we split mind into This and That, and discover that the part we live in is too small. When we divide mind into This and That, we limit our freedom.

Now suppose that we only divided the yard out of fear that the chickens and the dog wouldn't get along. But what if they do? What if when we put them together they get along just fine? This is like realizing that This and That are inseparable. When we realize their inseparability, there is more room for both.

Now let's say that when we separate the chickens and the dog, the dog becomes fascinated by the chickens, charges the fence, and terrifies them; but when we put them together, they get to know each other and relax. Similarly, when This and That come together in egolessness, the passion, aggression, and ignorance resulting from their interaction stops.

The dog and chickens analogy demonstrates why we need to see the truth about This and That: when we do, like the dog and the chickens, we experience a lot less tension and a lot more freedom. However, the analogy breaks down in some respects. The dog and the chickens still remain enclosed even when put together, but when This meets That the space becomes limitless. Also, the chickens never become a dog, but That does become This and vice versa. At a certain point on the path, we actually do become our computer screen, keyboard, living room furniture, and everything else in our world. They are no longer separate from us; they are us. As a result, we experience a delightful, frictionless world.

We develop an understanding of the illusoriness of This and That through a long series of insights. The first is the absence of This—self, or ego. In my case, I first experienced nonego when I asked myself a question and found no one there to answer. (Some say we are insane if we answer when we talk to ourselves, but what are we when we talk to ourselves and there is no one to answer?)

It may be appropriate here to say a few words about my writing about what "I" have experienced on the path, which could seem boastful as well as being misleading. To clarify, from the moment we discover there is no self, "I" no longer has a part on the spiritual path. However, the word "I," and other flawed words like it, are the most natural way to communicate in a dualistic language that requires an actor, an act, and often someone or something that is the act's recipient. The true feeling of the Dharma is something like "undifferentiated emptiness inseparable from awareness of itself dwells without anyone or anything doing or receiving it," which makes for tiresome reading, at least in English.

Also, I relate my personal experiences to be of help, and hope the reader will view my writing in this spirit and not as an attempt to proclaim "my" progress.

To continue, the second insight is that That, or other, is also absent. We may wonder why this process occurs stepwise: knowing that This and That arise simultaneously, we might expect them to cease simultaneously. All I can say is that it doesn't work that way. In my case, years passed between my first experience of the absence of This and my realization of the egolessness or unreality of That. Furthermore, before seeing through That, I still acted as though This existed. My behavior was a product of old habits, sometimes called karma or habitual patterns. For a long time—some speak of kalpas, which is so much time it's not even worth talking about—we have been viewing the world from the standpoint of ego. As a result, we have developed strong reflexes which remain long after ego itself disappears. In other words, although we may thoroughly realize that there is no This, we continue to relate to the world as if there were. For that reason, for the sake of both This and That, we must also realize the egolessness of That.

Both meditation and daily life help us to see that That is not real. Part of Mahayana Buddhism is the slogan, "Regard all dharmas as dreams." "Dharmas," in this case, are everything that constitutes what we believe to be other. This slogan prepares us for the time when we *experience* all dharmas as dreams: when we see that the world truly has no inherent existence, is not based on anything—is, in other words, egoless or dreamlike. At that point, we remove the sting of That, and its power to trigger the reflex of This.

Once we have seen both This and That to be egoless, we still have further to go, because we have yet to see that their egolessness is the same. We will need more time to realize that the nothingness of This is precisely the same as the unreality of That. Such was my confusion for about a year, until sitting in my meditation hut one day I looked at a small table and discovered that its unreality had the same quality as my experience of the absence of self. They were the same in their egolessness.

At this stage, we still have not resolved This and That completely. The realization that This and That are not two creates a limitless space in consciousness, but unfortunately, as humans will, we tend to grasp on to that discovery rather than simply allowing it to unfold. Even at this stage of insight, something persists, subtly, to be aware of the limitless space. Whatever it is must dissolve before limitless space can truly be experienced.

Even after that dissolution, we are still not completely finished with the duality of This and That. In spite of the fact that we now experience—without an experiencer, observer, or ego—a limitless space, we still have not fully opened to our freedom. We are like a zoo lion that has been caged all its life and then taken into the wild. The lion's cage is open, but the lion remains inside because it has not fully understood the possibilities of its freedom. Held by the security of the cage and fear of the unknown, the animal hesitates to explore the boundless freedom outside the cage. Although our freedom is limitless, we still have not committed ourselves to it. When we do, we take the final step: we finally resolve and dissolve This and That.

MEDITATION BEFORE REALIZATION

*When emotions arise, we observe them, and we develop
means to keep them from carrying us away, although we
still have strong habitual tendencies to the contrary.*

A lot has been written about Buddhist meditation. More
than a lot, actually: every Buddhist teacher of repute has
taught about it. (Two of my favorites from this body of
teachings are Shunryu Suzuki Roshi's classic, *Zen Mind, Beginner's Mind,* and Milarepa's songs about meditation in *The
Hundred Thousand Songs of Milarepa.*) Since meditation has
been discussed so much, perhaps a new approach would
be helpful. The next three entries discuss how meditation
differs between practitioners who have and who have not
experienced realization. We can use this information to
evaluate where we are at present, and where we have to go.

There are many forms of meditation, particularly in Vajrayana Buddhism. Here, however, I will discuss only one practice common to all forms of Buddhism: mindfulness-awareness practice, also called the sitting practice of meditation.

For a very long time after being taught how to meditate, many of us will practice what could be called a mechanical approach to sitting meditation: we follow our breath to stay in the present, and label our thoughts as leverage to recognize when we had been lost in thought or emotion. What we experience while undistracted is limited, usually just a short glimpse of ourselves breathing, and is accompanied by a strong sense that someone or something is doing our breathing and having our thoughts, emotions, and experiences. We expend a lot of effort attempting to follow the technique, but thoughts and emotions frustrate us with constant intrusions. After leaving the breath, we black out for varying periods of time, lost in chains of thought. With prolonged sitting, our body hurts; coupled with the frustration we feel, this tends to make lengthy sitting uncomfortable.

Over time our practice changes, even prior to realization. With time, we learn to relax with the occurrences of mind, and to move from rigid attention to our breath to a more expansive appreciation of the space around it. This evolution from the close attention of mindfulness to the greater spaciousness of awareness opens us to our environment, and we hear the wind blow, rain tap, and birds sing. We become more relaxed about practice, expect less from it, and start to do it for its own sake. After meditation sessions, we also become more aware of our minds. When emotions arise, we observe them, and we develop means to keep them from carrying us away, although we still have strong habitual tendencies to the contrary. In fact, having become more comfortable with mind, we sometimes become too generous with our neuroses, mistakenly interpreting them as acts of freedom; this is a trap to be avoided. Since meditation opens us more, energies from the world become more vivid as well, but we still lack the skillful means to process them completely.

This is a brief sketch of meditation before realization.

MEDITATION AFTER
REALIZATION

---

*The occurrences of mind now pass like ownerless
planets cruising through space. No entity guides them.
They happen because that's what they do.*

This section examines meditation practice after realization. Realization is the experience of the empty/aware nature of mind. When we have that experience, we enter the Path of Seeing in Buddhism, and are said to be "realized" or to have the "view" of the true nature of reality.

Our meditation practice changes considerably with the discovery of the true nature of mind. Thoughts appear in a different light. Before, they were messages that tended to fascinate us; now they are glimpses of emptiness. Having realized the emptiness of mind, we now discover that thoughts are as empty as the mind they arise in. As a result, they float like snowflakes through mind and quickly dissolve into the emptiness they share with it. Every thought becomes a portal to realization.

These discoveries reduce the persuasiveness of thoughts considerably. In the limitless mental space revealed by realizing the absence of self and the groundlessness of phenomena, thoughts no longer feel so close to us and their messages influence us less. Also, we now possess (actually, are) an openness which is spontaneous and without need for maintenance. We can open effortlessly to thoughts and all other occurrences of mind and see them as simply occurrences—nothing more. Doing so strips them of their attention-grabbing credentials.

We approach emotions—thoughts with energy—in the same way. (To be accurate, at this level we don't actually approach anything: it simply happens.) We pacify strong thoughts and emotions by knowing they are not ours, since there is no one to have them. The occurrences of mind now pass like ownerless planets cruising through space. No entity guides them. They happen because that's what they do.

Awareness also takes on new qualities. Before realization, we felt that it was ours, something like a flashlight we directed at things. Now, without an I, awareness is no longer anyone's. It is self-existing and undirected. What were once our breath and bodily sensations have stopped being ours; they are now occurrences in awareness, with no greater value than a honking car or the kitchen sink. In meditation, we simply let awareness be as it is—or, more to the point, it is as it is. Also, since it is everywhere, there is no possibility of directing it. It has become an empty, ownerless appreciation that extends throughout limitless space, and feels (without a feeler) like it has always been and always will be.

Finally, with realization, meditation becomes the meditator and vice versa. Meditation is no longer something we do: it is what we are. No separation exists between us and anything else, including meditation, because there is no longer any self to be separate. Furthermore, we have progressed beyond merely seeing the absence of self to knowing that the emptiness we have become is indivisible, not split into inside and outside of us. Since meditation has become what we are, "trying" to be it no longer makes sense, so it becomes effortless. We do continue to meditate, though, because we still drift into chains of thoughts and emotions, although they now interfere less with the realization that has become our meditation.

In summary, after realization, meditation no longer requires effort. It is what we are and always have been, empty/awareness. Instead of being work, meditation practice is now bliss, because it connects us with the bliss of realization. In postmeditation, our life incorporates more of the realized state, this being the purpose of practice and the reason it's called "practice": we practice to bring the fruitions of meditation to everyday life. At this point, we are well along the way, but we still need meditation to stabilize realization into enlightenment.

MEDITATION WITH VISUALIZATION

With realization one discovers that the importance of the deity is not so much what it wears, but what it is: an anthropomorphic representation of emptiness.

Visualization practice is a form of meditation used in Vajrayana Buddhism. Generally speaking, the practice consists of forming a picture in one's mind of a deity—a humanlike entity, usually dressed in ancient Indian garb and accoutrements. Each deity represents an aspect of the mind of realization. For example, a female deity may carry a knife to cut through passion, or a male one a bowl of flaming jewels to demonstrate his protection of the Buddha, Dharma, and Sangha. The idea is that by visualizing a deity, the practitioner can connect with the aspect of realized mind it represents. Chögyam Trungpa once said the practice is like visualizing the yellow cabs, lights, and crowds of New York City in order to connect with the city's ambiance.

Because every detail of a deity signifies a spiritual achievement, a lot of emphasis is placed on visualizing them totally—not so easy when they have jewelry and various other objects (including weapons) on their bodies, and sometimes extra arms and heads. Usually, one also recites a mantra while doing the visualization to keep one's mind from straying into confusion, and to receive the special powers that mantras confer. For most practitioners, visualization practice consists of visualizing a deity separate from themselves in the hopes of gaining its power, while saying a chant to keep their mind from drifting into thoughts and emotions. After the visualization, they generally finish the practice with sitting meditation in an attempt to discover the aspect of mind the visualization has highlighted.

This is a general picture of visualization practice before the first experience of realization. (Actually, to speak of visualization practice before realization is somewhat problematic, because emptiness, an aspect of realization, is the experiential prerequisite for receiving a deity practice in the Vajrayana. In truth, however, very few people begin visualization practice with that level of insight; most come to the practice after fulfilling the necessary meditation and study requirements.) As with mindfulness-awareness meditation, visualization practice changes considerably with the experience of realization. In fact, only after that insight does one truly understand how the practice works.

Let's start with the deity itself. The deity is a picture created by mind. Crucially, this picture is empty, without thingness or substance, as are all occurrences of mind. The practitioner is encouraged to see all aspects of the deity, but with realization one discovers that the importance of the deity is not so much what it wears, but what it is: an anthropomorphic representation of emptiness.

Furthermore, because mind creates occurrences very much like visualizations all the time, visualization practice shows us that the occurrences of mind, such as thoughts, are also empty like the deity. In some visualization practices, we create an image both in front and inside of us. After experiencing realization, we understand that doing this helps us connect with the emptiness of the deity both inside and outside. That connection, in turn, conditions us to appreciate both the world and ourselves as empty, and prepares us for nonduality, the experience that the emptiness "inside" and the emptiness "outside" are one and the same.

I used to work as a medical researcher. I remember the feeling I often got when someone made a breakthrough: it seemed so simple that I wondered why I hadn't come up with it myself. Over time, however, I realized that breakthroughs are simple after the fact, but not before.

This is also true in the Dharma. Visualization practice is a highly effective training tool that helps one progress toward experiencing the nature of mind directly. It is a given that visualizations (even in the mundane sense, as when we conjure up a mental picture of our childhood home) arise in the mind's eye, and not in our regular eyes. Similarly, a remembered song would be heard by the mind's ear, and so on. These mental faculties constitute the awareness of mind spoken of in Buddhism. All this seems relatively straightforward, but what is not so straightforward is what this awareness of mind *feels* like. That's where we need a breakthrough, and that's where visualizations help. Each time we use the mind's eye to produce a visualization, it becomes more prominent and noticeable, like a muscle we build lifting weights. Eventually, it becomes so prominent that we finally experience its nature directly, including the nature of awareness. Visualization practices reveal the emptiness and awareness of mind, and help us connect with nonduality. We gain this understanding of the practices after realization. But do visualization practices lead to realization? In my experience, the answer is no. I did not make any major breakthroughs while actually doing visualization practices, although they may have prepared my mind for the insights that occurred in postmeditation.

What, then, is the place of visualizations after realization? In my case, I no longer do them, only mindfulness-awareness meditation. Teachers of the past support this choice. For example, the teachings on the complete path to Mahamudra in the great Buddhist text *Mahamudra* by Takpo Tashi Namgyal mention only the sitting practice of meditation, and my teacher and others have taught that sitting practice is the most advanced form of Vajrayana practice, suggesting its importance after realization. This makes sense to me: I no longer need intermediaries such as visualizations to lead me to insight, and I find using them actually interferes with it, just as a competent swimmer might find diagrams illustrating the correct positions in swimming unhelpful, because they give an imperfect impression of the actual swimming experience.

There seems to be an inconsistency with visualizations: the only experiential preparation for doing them is the realization of emptiness, while after realization I and many past teachers recommend the sitting practice of meditation. (As a caveat, some teachers do admonish their students not to abandon deity practice after experiencing realization. Also, as I change practices through the years, I always feel that the practice I am presently doing is superior to others. This was written at one point in time; at another point, my opinion may well change.)

So when do we do visualizations? We do them when most people do them, after fulfilling the necessary practice and study criteria. If we happen to experience realization before or after visualization practice, we let realization decide what practice to do next.

IGNORANCE

There is something that cuts through our ignorance about life. It is so immediate and real that it burns through all our concepts. When the Buddha attained enlightenment, he talked about it first. It is pain.

I'm getting old. I look it and I feel it. I talk to other aging people, and they yearn to be young: they are embarrassed about their age. The whole of society is attuned to youth. Youth is in; old age is out, repulsive, something to be hidden with cosmetics and cosmetic surgery. I, however, have no desire to be young, for a very simple reason: I never want to be that dumb again.

I was dumb about many things in life, and I caused a lot of pain for myself and others. Looking back, it seems my stupidity arose not so much from the conditions I faced in life, which admittedly weren't good, but from my ignorance of the nature of life itself: who or what lives life, what is lived, and the difference, if any, between the two. Since I spent a lot of time and effort answering those questions, it seems quite natural that I do not wish to return to the ignorance of my youth. I suspect that aging people who wish to be young again may never have asked those fundamental questions, or enjoyed the pleasure age brings in answering them.

With anything in life, if we don't relate to it, we never learn about it, and we suffer the consequences. If our toilet makes a noise and we refuse to examine it, we end up calling a plumber and paying a sizable bill. At present, the world is going through a serious economic recession because supposedly sophisticated money managers purchased complex securities without knowing what they contained. They didn't take the time to inspect what they bought, and people throughout the world are paying the price.

Ignorance of life itself is like ignorance of most topics, but is easier to maintain. We ignore our lives all the time. If we look carefully, we find that everything we do other than being aware of our living and breathing can be a way to hand our life over to something else. If watching television, talking, reading, or thinking blacks us out to the world before our eyes, we are choosing those activities over awareness of our life. Our eyes are open every moment we are awake, but how much do we actually see? At home, when our gaze falls on the carpet or dining room table, do we actually see those things? Walking outside, when we look down at the pavement, do we actually see it? Are we truly in touch with what passes before our eyes, or are we somewhere else, caught up in our thoughts and emotions? We could say that thoughts and emotions are parts of life too, but that is only true if we notice them—and how often do we do that? If we are truly in touch with our life, we should recognize each time we think, and it shouldn't distract us from the world around us.

Because we fail to pay attention to life, we learn very little about it. Few of us know who or what lives it, taking for granted that it is an entity called "me" and never stopping to check if there is such a thing. We also take the world for granted, never considering that it could have a reality other than what most people believe.

There is something that cuts through our ignorance about life. It is so immediate and real that it burns through all our concepts. When the Buddha attained enlightenment, he talked about it first. It is pain. Our ignorance of who we are and the nature of the world we live in exposes us and others to pain. If we think we are a solid entity who must adjust a solid world to its needs, we will suffer pain. If we perceive others as separate from ourselves—as entities to grasp, reject, or ignore—they will suffer pain as well. Pain alerts us when we are missing the point about life, and it can also lead us out of ignorance. It can show us the nature of reality, because it is real: we cannot conceptualize our way out of it. We are going to suffer pain in life; there is no doubt about that, so why not acknowledge it and use it to free ourselves from ignorance?

Pain is one reason to examine life, and another is the sadness inherent in living in a system we never understand. As Socrates said, "The unexamined life is not worth living." To spend our whole life ignorant of its meaning (or lack thereof), to live without ever understanding what we have lived, is a tragedy. For me, cluelessness about anything is one of the saddest aspects of human existence, and especially if it is about life itself.

In Buddhism, a human life is regarded as precious. First, it is not easy being born a human: there are an estimated one with nineteen zeros insects on the earth, so it is a lot easier to be born a hornet than *Homo sapiens*. The more substantial reason is that only as humans can we transcend our ignorance about how life really works. If we return as anything else, we lose access to the insight only humans can acquire.

Buddhism, the teachings and practices of the Buddha, is the only way to dispel our fundamental ignorance about life. It teaches us to question who we are and where we are, and it emphasizes being here and now, the only place where those questions can be answered.

Sense of Humor

A sense of humor is not necessarily laughing out loud,
making jokes, or being the life of the party. A sense
of humor is touching the infinite space of mind.

There is a story in Tibet about a monk who kept an expensive piece of turquoise on his shrine for a rainy day. One day, while the monk was meditating, a mouse appeared on the shrine and started pulling the turquoise toward a hole. Try as he might, the mouse could not accomplish the task: the turquoise was too heavy. Another mouse came to his assistance, and together they pulled the turquoise into the hole. At that moment, the monk burst into laughter and attained realization.

Recently, I had a similar experience. Many of us have a fear that surpasses all others; mine is being sued for negligence as a physician. It isn't about the financial damage, which can be considerable, but about being perceived as incompetent, uncaring, or a failure. My fear drives me to keep precise records and to practice medicine and approach my patients in a way that prevents lawsuits.

I had a patient with fibromyalgia, a nagging muscular pain syndrome that is difficult to treat. It doesn't kill you, but it can make you wish you were dead. I had tried my patient on various therapies without success when, on one visit, he brought in an article about a new drug for fibromyalgia. Although it wasn't approved by the FDA, many people had attested to its effectiveness, so after discussing the side effects with him, I agreed to try it.

My patient did great on the drug for about two years, then walked into my office one day, told me he had lost everything gambling, and showed me several articles linking the drug to compulsive gambling. Immediately, the possibility of a lawsuit flashed into my mind. I had given him a drug that was not yet cleared for his problem, and it had ruined his life. I knew that people often sue because of money worries, and this man was completely broke. I felt a surge of anxiety; my worst fear was coming to life. And then something happened, something I had never before done in similar circumstances: I smiled. And that smile made all the difference to me.

Many of us might not consider a sense of humor to be part of spirituality. Spirituality is serious, holy, sacred, steeped in tradition. It deals with serious issues like God, death, and the afterlife, and it never fails to remind us what will happen to us if we don't take those issues seriously.

Religion is so serious that millions have been tortured and killed in its name. However, I was taught by a buddha, and he encouraged me to have a sense of humor and said it was an important part of spirituality. When I smiled, I understood why. I saw how a sense of humor helps us let go of impossible expectations, such as living in a completely secure world. I had done everything I could to protect myself from lawsuits, yet an unexpected side-effect negated all my efforts. The two mice had carried my turquoise away. The absurdity of what had happened and the complete hopelessness I felt in the face of another of life's tricks made me smile. Who did I think I was, and what did I think the world was? When was I going to get the point? We can only do so much; the rest is out of our control. At some point we have to give up the illusion that we can control this capricious life, and smile. After all, no matter how successfully we manage it, life is going to kill us. (As for my patient, he and I were able to work successfully with his medical and gambling problems, and a lawsuit never materialized. As for myself, a simple smile saved me a lot of worry.)

Like so much in the Dharma, humor can't be created. We all know people who force humor on us—and who, if they choose me as their audience, do so at the risk of their lives (a little humor there). True humor, like a true smile, arises without effort. A sense of humor is not necessarily laughing out loud, making jokes, or being the life of the party. A sense of humor is touching the infinite space of mind.

For a long time, I practiced meditation with all the tools realization offered, but without a real sense of bliss. When I smiled, I found out why: I needed a better sense of humor. The Dharma is about bringing more and more of mind's space into our lives. As we progress on the path, that space enlarges until it becomes limitless. I had experienced that limitless space, but smiling showed me how to fully apply it. When I smiled, I saw how to connect life's trials with the space that we are—in other words, the value of a sense of humor.

I remember a time when we all talked about people being "uptight," when the accepted approach to life was to "stay loose." After I smiled, I remembered those old phrases, and appreciated their wisdom. Being uptight means missing the space around situations; from an enlightened standpoint, it means missing the limitless space of mind. When tension builds in us, we can deflate it into the space of mind, but when we hold on to our sense of being threatened, we miss that space and our fear becomes our whole world. When I smiled, I felt my uptightness merge with that limitless space.

A chant I have always loved extolling the virtues of a buddha says, "He has completely cut the knots." There are countless knots to cut, and many we don't even realize we have. On the day I smiled, I found the knot of humorlessness and how to cut it with a sense of humor.

MEANING

Contrary to what many believe,
a life without meaning is quite pleasant.

For millennia, philosophers and people in general have pondered the meaning of life. A minority have even considered that it has none, an idea many find repulsive. Perhaps a meaningless life seems like a wasteland, stretching on and on without any landmarks to tell where we are or how we are doing. Our need for confirmation reminds me of a story about Mae West, a woman known for ribald frankness, who had mirrors on the ceiling of her bedroom. When asked what they were for, she responded, "I like to see how I'm doing."

Chögyam Trungpa once said, "There is no meaning, but there is truth." The mind of realization, which was his entire life, exists without meaning. It simply observes—quite keenly, I might add—without jumping to conclusions, including the conclusion that what it observes has meaning. Incidentally, my teacher's statement also indicates that truth is more important than meaning. In other words, we should not feel discouraged about losing meaning, if its loss is a greater truth.

Ego creates meaning in order to exist. Ego is simply a creation of our mind, with no substantive existence; at any moment, it might dissolve into the nothingness of mind itself. Its insubstantiality makes us insecure, so we search for ways to solidify it. One of those ways is meaning, which grants ego the dual status of creating it and of being its moderator. Anything that enhances the world's importance enhances ego's position as responder to that importance.

We may find it a stretch to dismiss meaning. After all, how can such things as raising children, helping others, and living an exemplary life be without meaning? Bodhidharma, the Indian monk who founded Chán Buddhism in China, was once called before the Chinese emperor, who asked if the benevolent things he had done for his people entitled him to Buddhist realization. Bodhidharma responded that the emperor's activities didn't entitle him to anything, and that a truly meritorious deed in Buddhism, the attainment of insight, is beyond the grasp of human intelligence—in other words, beyond any of the constructs of mind, such as the meaningfulness of the emperor's munificence. It was a dangerous comment to make to an emperor, especially one puffed up with virtuousness, but Bodhidharma's willingness to undercut meaning showed that his realization was valid, and that not even the risk of being put to death could persuade him to abandon it.

Contrary to what many believe, a life without meaning is quite pleasant. Meaning clutters life, and makes it heavy and sluggish, like a bureaucracy. In fact, meaning *is* a bureaucracy. We apply the Bureau of Meaning's stamp to everything we encounter, robbing life of its vividness, spontaneity, and playfulness—its effortless bliss.

Life has no meaning, and we can enjoy it much more when we experience that fact. The process is not easy, but we can begin simply: we can ask ourselves what meaning exists in life besides what we give it. If we look at meaning in that way, we can begin to see the possibility that it is simply our creation, not an intrinsic part of life.

SMART

One thing I have learned is that smart isn't wise.

I have always wanted to be smart. I'm not dumb, but I'm not as smart as I would like to be.

In my lineage of Buddhism, when one takes refuge, formally committing oneself to the Buddhist path, one receives a name that signifies one's strongest attribute. At my interview with my teacher before receiving this name, I wore a blue tie, because blue is associated with intellect in Tibetan Buddhism. I hoped to trick my teacher into giving me an "intellect" name—which was a really dumb idea, because having such a name wouldn't have made me smarter, and my teacher couldn't be tricked. (He gave me a "discipline" name.) Anyhow, this little vignette demonstrates how badly I wanted to be smart.

There are many advantages to being smart. Intelligence has always been important, and it seems more so in modern times: intelligent people gain entrance to the right schools, leading to the contacts and credentials that make for a comfortable life. The balance seems to have shifted especially dramatically for men. No one needs a hunter or fighter anymore; most men's strength is used mainly to open jars.

Smart people also have advantages in the Dharma. People recognize intelligence much more readily than they do realization, so smart people are chosen as teachers. Conversely, one might experience realization but still be excluded from teaching because of a lack of facility with words or concepts. Some who *are* the Dharma go unnoticed, while those who teach it have the good fortune to share it with others.

I have spent a lot of time around smart people. I have a lot of education, and smart people teach. My work as a physician brings me in touch with colleagues who are often quite smart. I am also married to an intelligent woman and have a similarly gifted son (in their cases, I'm talking about Ivy League and MENSA-smart). I have been with enough intelligent people that I know not only the benefits of intelligence, but also the drawbacks.

One thing I have learned is that smart isn't wise. I have known many highly intelligent people who did very dumb things in life. Because society rewards their gifts so lavishly, intelligent people have a tendency to become arrogant, which can be their undoing. I once read a book entitled *The Best and the Brightest* about the very intelligent people who ran America during the Vietnam War and the problems they caused with their arrogance and lack of wisdom. From many similar accounts of other periods, the evidence is conclusive: being bright is no guarantee of getting it right.

Intelligence also has a number of drawbacks in the Dharma. Brains alone aren't enough on the path to enlightenment: even a rocket scientist can't figure it out. The fruitions of the path don't fall into anyone's lap; even very intelligent people have to exert a lot more effort than simply thinking about them. In fact, since realization occurs when all concept stops, too much facility with concept can hinder one's progress.

Smart people are also at a disadvantage in the Dharma because they see things coming. They anticipate problems—something I have never been guilty of. They notice and sidestep challenges to their ego, when those challenges could lead to realization, as in the following story. I met a teacher, not my root guru, whom intelligent people warned me about. I discounted what they said and became very attached to him. Eventually I got the ax, as they had foreseen, and I suffered a broken heart that brought me to realization. If I had listened to the smart guys, I would have been spared the pain, but I would have missed the opportunity for the realization that followed. It helps to be a little dumb in the Dharma, dumb enough to stick your ego out far enough to get its head chopped off.

In some ways, being realized is like being intelligent. When my wife or son understands something I don't, I can't see the trick no matter how hard I try. I have suffered with intelligent people that way all my life. Now I understand how it feels to be on their side of the fence. I find smart people as helpless to fathom the insights of realization as all others—maybe more so. Smart people are often better at figuring things out than feeling them, but realization must be felt. Their concepts take them further from rather than closer to the experience. Please don't get me wrong: I am saddened when anyone doesn't experience the Dharma. With brainiacs, however, who may have more advantages and arrogance than regular folks, I do sometimes find it more healthy than saddening when they have to work at it a bit.

Very intelligent people have attained realization, one example being my teacher. I remember believing that if I ever attained it I would become as smart as him. It hasn't happened yet. Realization reveals the nature of mind; it doesn't make an individual mind smarter. I'm still as helpless in the face of higher mathematics as always. Naropa was another very intelligent Buddhist, maybe one of the smartest men of his time. He too became enlightened, but he went through hell with his teacher Tilopa before he finally penetrated through the dense layers of concept that only a towering intellect can accumulate.

Although I never became the brain I wanted to be, I did discover other aptitudes, such as commitment, courage, and openness. As a result, I eventually stumbled onto one pretty smart conclusion: the best thing to achieve in life is not what we want, but what we are.

ENERGY

The best way to use energy in the Dharma is to grasp.

Today is the last day of the Dön Season, a time of year in Tibetan Buddhism when particularly high energies are said to circulate in the world. During this season, practitioners are encouraged to keep a low profile, since in the heightened energy small mistakes tend to balloon into big ones. I had an elderly lady in the hospital during a Dön Season some years ago, and one night I received several calls from the nurses saying she wasn't feeling well. It was late and I was tired, so instead of going in to see her, I treated her over the phone. Several hours later, I got a call informing me she had died. I was devastated. Every Dön Season, I remember her and how I felt during that time. As a result, I always do the appropriate seasonal chants and carefully watch my affairs when the Dön Season rolls around.

I have a lot of energy. I have used it successfully in sports, academics, medicine, interpersonal relationships, and the Dharma. Of all those areas, it has really benefited me most in the Dharma, since it interfaces so nicely with my inability to see things coming. I crash into situations at high speed; some almost kill me, and others bring me to piercing insights. It's like jumping horses, a high-energy sport I enjoy. Jumping a horse is unlike playing golf for many reasons, the main one being the cost of making a mistake. If we hit a bad golf shot, we are penalized strokes, but if we make an error jumping, our body is penalized, and maybe our life. A mistake jumping a horse is always an illuminating experience, one we never forget.

The best way to use energy in the Dharma is to grasp. This may seem perverse, since all Dharma is based on giving up grasping or wanting. But almost everything we do before realization involves grasping, so if we are stuck with it, why not use it? Why not grasp something—a lover, a career, or the hope of attaining enlightenment—with as much energy as possible, the better to quickly feel the pain and futility associated with doing so?

Strong grasping can lead to realization. Let's say we grip a rope weakly and get pulled up a few feet before letting go. It's no big deal. But if we grip the rope hard and get pulled up a thousand feet before letting go, we experience a big free fall, an enlightening experience. It's the same thing as climbing up and walking off the "ten-thousand-foot pole" often talked about in Zen.

Many people are afraid of energy, and with reason: it can be dangerous to body and mind. I tend to like it, though, something I learned from playing sports as a youth and adult. Most athletes feel "butterflies" before competing, which over time they learn to channel into productive play. I learned to do that, and discovered how wonderful it was to convert fear into success. Later in life, I discovered that Vajrayana Buddhism specializes in the same conversion, though its practitioners' intent is not to compete at a high level but to help others.

My teacher, a great Vajrayana practitioner, taught that emotions are simply thoughts with energy that we can learn to flip into the space of realization, extracting their energies to benefit others in the process. Vajrayana practices have been developed to teach us to do just that. Of course, nothing is as easy as it sounds: if we still have vestiges of ego and try to flip emotions, we fry. This is why the experiential preparation for the Vajrayana is emptiness, the complete absence of ego. If we have a sense of self and attempt to play with energies, the two rub together until our mind catches fire with fear, lust, depression, or whatever our tendencies toward mental instability are. We get cooked.

Our world is filled with energies of all kinds. They can lead us and others to enlightenment, or they can be misused and entrench us in wanting, rejecting, and ignoring. It all depends on how we work with them.

DEPRESSION

I think of depression as reverse enlightenment.

For much of my adult life, I worked two jobs. One was the practice of medicine, and the other was managing major depression. Unlike some people, I did both jobs at the same time.

I had depression for twenty-five years before I knew it, although I frequently diagnosed it in my patients. One wonders how a physician could miss his own diagnosis for so long, after learning about it in training and observing it in patients. Such is the insidious nature of depression: I was unable to step outside it for a more objective view, and so I accepted it as who I was, not as a problem. Until I made my own diagnosis, I believed everyone felt as I did (which was true in some sense, since healthy people also have periods of feeling down). And I was not the only one fooled. I recall only one person telling me I was the most serious person she had ever met—a possible hint. No physicians, in all the years I worked and associated with them, ever suggested I might be depressed.

There is a very old English saying: "It's an ill wind that blows no good." It is apt for depression, especially with regard to the Dharma. The Buddha's first teaching is that life is pervaded with suffering. No one will need to force-feed that truth to someone suffering from depression, a pain so great that people kill themselves to escape it. The pain of major depression, in particular, contains the most toxic mixture of mental states known to man, among them fear, insecurity, worthlessness, hopelessness, lack of energy, inability to sleep or eat, and, not surprisingly, an inability to enjoy life. Small wonder, then, that when I heard the Buddha taught "life is pain," I knew I was meant to be a Buddhist, and when I heard he also taught how to transcend that pain, I was hooked for life. I could not have found a better preparation for the Dharma than depression.

A proviso is in order: as a physician, I believe and practice that everyone suffering from serious depression should receive medication. Nothing works as effectively or quickly as medication, and depression is a life-threatening disease that must be treated as soon as possible. No time should be wasted on counseling, psychotherapy, or religious approaches—including the Dharma—in lieu of drugs. Patients need medication immediately to preserve their lives. Other modalities can be employed after survival has been assured.

I treated my depression for ten years with only Buddhist meditation. My teacher was a buddha and possessed all the insights of one, but he never told me I had depression and should treat it. He was an expert in enlightenment, not Western medicine. (In fairness to him, I do remember him saying to a group, while looking pointedly at me, "Don't commit suicide—there is more to come.") Meditation worked well for two years when I lived in a meditation center and practiced five hours a day, but failed when I returned to the stresses of the world and greatly reduced practice time. To persist using only Buddhism was extremely dangerous, and medication saved my life. That is why I insist that my depressed patients take medication first before turning to secondary approaches, such as spirituality.

I'm closing the clinic now, and returning to the ways depression can assist us in the Dharma. I think of depression as reverse enlightenment. On the path to enlightenment, we experience an increasing spaciousness of mind that eventually becomes limitless. With depression, we go the other way: we lose any spaciousness whatsoever, and collapse into a dense core of pain, a black hole that sucks up our awareness, joy, and humor. This exaggerated loss of spaciousness can be instructive. If we know the Dharma and then take medication, we can experience our recovery as a quick unfolding of the Buddhist path. In my case, two weeks after I began taking medication, my mental space began to increase, and I experienced an unfolding of the truth of the Dharma. Eventually, I sat on my couch and spontaneously uttered, "Lord of Centerless Space," a segment of a Buddhist chant outlining the qualities of an enlightened person, so profound was my experience with the medication. I hadn't completely experienced the nature of the space I described, but I had contacted it. It was an amazing testament to the truth of the Dharma when my sanity returned as stages on the Buddhist path.

Almost all people with depression have chronic anxiety. In fact, I can't think of an exception among all my patients with depression. Of all the symptoms of my depression, pervasive anxiety was the most painful. The severity and length of my suffering from anxiety taught me to abhor it, so I will not rhapsodize about it except to say that even it has benefits in the Dharma. Chögyam Trungpa once said that a Vajrayana practitioner should panic frequently, because at some point he or she might see the other side of panic. My own fear was so pervasive that I never saw the other side, until I received medication. Then I understood the power and insight he was describing. Now I know that I and my world—including fear—are empty, and that fear's energy makes it a particularly good way to connect with that emptiness. In fact, one of the reasons I still practice medicine is for the energies it creates in me, including fear. There is a point on the path when our most difficult emotions evolve into our best means for progress.

At this point, I know both major depression and the Dharma in my bones, as they say in Zen. I have been involved with each for a long time, and I now see them as both opposite poles of mind and the same pole. This seemingly absurd statement will make sense to people with depression who prevent it from ruining their life for long enough to appreciate it as a manifestation of realization. In other words, don't commit suicide—there is more to come.

STUCK

Realization is not a belief system,
a way of thinking, or the result of logic.

There once was a king who ruled a country where the water made his subjects insane. To preserve his sanity, he drank water from a private reserve for a time, but his sanity made him incomprehensible to his countrymen. After a while, he could no longer tolerate being separate from them, so he drank the water of insanity.

If we have found attainment on the Buddhist path, we too may long for a world where everyone shares our understanding. But unlike the king, realized people are unable to change. They *are* realization. They are stuck: when they look at themselves and the world, they see only what they have realized.

I remember being at a talk given by Chögyam Trungpa where he was asked a question about himself. Most people asked him about the Dharma or how to deal with difficult life situations, so the query was unusual. There was a pause, and then he responded quizzically, "You mean, *me?*" He seemed puzzled by the question, which seldom happened: he had left the world of self so completely that he had to reflect for a moment on the premise of having one, and then try to respond appropriately. Amusingly, he had become stuck, unable to think outside enlightenment's box.

Realization is not a belief system, a way of thinking, or the result of logic. It is what we are. Even if we found the most elegant conceptual system, supported by impeccable logic, and decided to follow it, we couldn't after experiencing realization. We can't change who or what we have realized ourselves and the world to be, and if we try, we invite trouble. If we attempt to be solidly something, such as rude or uncaring, it is like shooting inappropriate ammunition from a rifle. You can only shoot emptiness bullets out of a realization rifle. Any other ammunition doesn't fit the chamber, and if we force it, we blow up the rifle and ourselves. If we attempt to solidify energies into a self and a world for it to manipulate, we explode.

Shunryu Suzuki Roshi said, "Even if the sun were to rise from the west, the bodhisattva has but one way." We might think this is because bodhisattvas have great will—and they do—but it is also because they are ruled by their accomplishment. They are beings who have reached a level of great compassion, and they can only act in accord with it. My first formal meeting with Chögyam Trungpa was when

I took refuge with him, committing myself to the Buddhist path. As I stood before him, I immediately experienced his mind, and found the pleasure so great that I wanted to stand there for the rest of my life. I understood then about the bliss of a buddha's mind, and remembered that only compassion can make them leave it and enter the chaos of our world. Even bodhisattvas and buddhas are stuck, in their case as instruments of compassion. We are fortunate that they are.

Not Appreciating Ourselves

Most of us, no matter how hard we try, are not going
to truly appreciate our self as long as we have one.

Chögyam Trungpa Rinpoche, my teacher, wrote an international bestseller called *Shambhala: The Sacred Path of the Warrior.* The second chapter begins, "A great deal of chaos in the
world occurs because people don't appreciate themselves."

Appreciating ourselves may seem easy to do, but in reality it requires years of effort. Most of us, no matter how
hard we try, are not going to truly appreciate our self as long
as we have one. Trying to maintain a self or to latch onto
things that confirm it makes us susceptible to the disappointments associated with any project.

Our notions of who we are cause us problems in many
ways. We may notice how uneasy we feel around others: we

aren't satisfied with ourselves, nor are they with themselves. This lack of appreciation forces us to tiptoe around, careful not to step on each other's psychological corns. We feel this interfere with our communication. It's like living in a totalitarian society where our mail is monitored, where we can't write what we wish for fear of rousing the authorities. I remember having felt these constraints for a long time before I heard a talk on psychological pain by Krishnamurti, a twentieth-century Indian sage. After an hour's discourse, he revealed that our awkwardness came from our belief in self, a disclosure that elicited a prolonged "Oh" from one who had experienced a lot of tiptoeing without knowing why.

Having defined ourselves by reference points, we often fail to appreciate even those. For example, many of us don't like our appearance. I observe people closely (a habit ingrained in me by a profession that diagnoses physical problems), and I often notice how people hesitate to expose their teeth when they smile, or turn their heads in certain ways to hide features that cause them discomfort. This discomfort translates into mine, so I know the prevalence of these problems from the years of uneasiness they have caused me.

Only when we discover what we really are, which is nothing, will we be truly equipped to deal with the chaos my teacher mentions. This discovery will take time, though, and in the meantime we need to find ways to become kinder to ourselves. The best way is through meditation. Many alternative approaches, such as the cures of the self-help industry, are simply bandages for a wound in need of more intensive care. We need more than stances toward accepting ourselves; we need to start doing it, and meditation provides that possibility. Meditation introduces us to our actual self, and allows us to study it along with the thoughts and emotions that influence it. It helps us make a relationship with self, not just throw nostrums at it. And once we've begun to understand self, meditation also gives us a chance at the cure—seeing through it entirely.

Ultimately, there's no substitute for the discovery that self is not real. In a sense, everything we do before this discovery is simply personality adjustment: different approaches to ego that end up reinforcing it. We must see through self in order to truly work with chaos, and the best way to do that is to meditate. By sitting and feeling the tension each of us calls "me," we eventually learn to relax with it. Self is just an occurrence of mind, no different from a thought or emotion. If we grow used to it, eventually it stops being an issue and becomes just "that old thing": me. Having heard all its claims and experienced all its highs and lows, we become bored with it. Without our attention sustaining it, it dissipates.

The easiest way to learn to like our self is to find we have none. Then the question of whether we like or dislike it no longer arises. That discovery isn't easy, though— most of us will need years of commitment to the teachings, teacher, and practices to accomplish it.

NOWHERE TO PUT IT

If we persist in meditation, at some
point we discover that our mental garbage
comes out of the vastness of mind.

Many years ago, the garbage collectors in New York City
went on strike. I remember seeing the pictures as the garbage quickly piled into mountains, covering the sidewalks
and streets. I don't remember how the strike was resolved,
but it became evident that it had to be settled quickly: the
refuse began replacing the living space, and the obstruction,
stench, and health hazard made the city unlivable. If New
York City's doctors, policemen, or firemen had gone on
strike, I don't think it could have posed a greater problem.

What happened in New York City commonly occurs
in our minds. As we age, we accumulate more and more of
what could be called mental garbage: disappointments, re-
sentments, missed opportunities, and memories of unpleasant

159

experiences we have endured or inflicted upon others. These begin piling up, and become so persistent and pervasive that eventually we accept them as who we are. We become our failures and judge ourselves accordingly.

People without effective meditation practices face two major problems in dealing with their mental garbage. First, they have typically never looked at it closely. Because they hesitate to relate to its smelly, gooey aspects, they haven't learned what it is or where it comes from. Second, even if they are aware of it, without access to the limitless nature of mind they can't eliminate it.

Meditation solves the first problem by providing us with an opportunity to study our garbage over and over. When we begin practicing meditation, we find ourselves preoccupied by self-centered thoughts and emotions, which is precisely what we have to examine. Meditation alerts us that our refuse is accumulating.

We solve the second problem through three general approaches, which together constitute the Buddhist path. Buddhism has been dealing with mental waste and its treatment for a long time, and the solutions it has found are organized into the path's Hinayana, Mahayana, and Vajrayana stages. The Hinayana practitioner seeks to avoid creating mental waste by living an austere life devoid of pollutants such as passion, aggression, and ignorance; and the Mahayana practitioner, having controlled his or her own garbage, then helps others to control theirs.

The Vajrayana approach to mental wastes is not unlike one of the methods proposed to handle nuclear wastes: to shoot them into space, after extracting their richest components for the benefit of others. This method for dealing with physical waste carries prohibitive costs and the censure of some of the planet's prominent citizens, who quail at the idea of polluting the universe. I find the idea appealing, however, since there are billions of solar systems in our galaxy, and billions of galaxies that no amount of waste from one tiny planet can pollute. I also find the Vajrayana approach to mental wastes—to see them in their true context of limitless space—helpful.

If we persist in meditation, at some point we discover that our mental garbage comes out of the vastness of mind. This discovery puts us on the way to mental sanitation, because the refuse not only arises from mind's limitless space, but returns to it as well: the whole system is a natural, sanitary cycle. When we become expert sanitation engineers, we also find that the garbage itself is space, and seeing it automatically puts it in its proper place. In other words, when seen correctly, our garbage is already sanitized.

At some point on the path, the refuse and where we put it become the same, so we create problems for ourselves if we try to send it elsewhere. If we sit and observe our garbage in meditation without trying to get rid of it, we will eventually and quite naturally discover that it's fine just where it is.

PRACTICE AND LIFE

It's best to allow practice to seep into our life, rather than force it. To apply it rather than being it is fraught with problems, as are all conceptual approaches to spirituality.

In Buddhism, life divides into meditation and postmeditation. During meditation, we endeavor to discover the true nature of mind. In postmeditation, we bring our discoveries to everyday life, working to be more in touch with them.

I first practiced Buddhism in the Zen tradition, where I found transitioning from meditation practice to everyday life quite difficult—so difficult, in fact, that I eventually abandoned Zen. The contrast between sitting and following one's breath in a quiet environment and navigating the speed and pressure of modern life proved too much to reconcile for a beginning practitioner like myself. Even in Tibetan Buddhism, which provides more tools for making the transition, I experienced difficulties. I recall finishing a solitary retreat and being amazed at how sensitive I had become. I was repulsed by the coarse way people seemed to approach their lives, talking loudly and quickly and seldom taking the time to engage meaningfully with each other. I felt open and raw, and when I faced brusqueness or superficiality, I deflated helplessly. The transition presented a real problem for me.

I have spent years trying to meld practice and life, and I sometimes lost sight of life in the process. On one occasion, I applied what I believed to be a meditative approach to an interview with a group of bureaucrats: one interviewer wanted to know why I had left one state to practice medicine in another, and, being open and truthful as a result of meditation, I replied that the reason involved my personal life and I felt the query was inappropriate. The interviewer responded by withholding a license I needed, causing me months of anxiety. I had forgotten, while attempting to apply practice to life, that in the real world people who protect the public sometimes need to ask personal questions—and that evading those questions, even while speaking from the spontaneity and openness of meditation, creates suspicion. I have learned the hard way never to lose sight of the realities of everyday life, no matter how lofty my spiritual sense may be.

I have also learned that it's best to allow practice to seep into our life, rather than force it. To *apply* it rather than *being* it is fraught with problems, as are all conceptual approaches to spirituality. Here and now is the best place to mix everyday life and practice; when we act based on schemata detached from the reality of the present moment, we court disaster.

In our endeavor to bridge practice and life, as in all things, nothing trumps experience. With time, greater insights into the nature of reality teach us how to properly combine the two. When practice shows us that the world is illusory, we no longer need to force onto life our concepts about it. When we experience the vastness of mind, energies begin to dissolve effortlessly into it, with no need for clunky, conceptual processes that lead to clunky results.

We finally resolve the practice/life dichotomy when we become the practice and it becomes us. At that point (a very advanced one), the struggle ceases. We are meditation and can be nothing else, and our approach to the world can only be a meditative one. At that point, we stride confidently through the "dusty world," now become a playground.

SPIRITUAL MATERIALISM

---

*No matter who we are, if we search for mind
rather than simply being it, we are caught
in the embrace of spiritual materialism.*

When Chögyam Trungpa first came to North America,
he devoted considerable attention to a problem he called
"spiritual materialism." In fact, he wrote a book called *Cutting Through Spiritual Materialism*. Spiritual materialism is the
use of spirituality in the service of ego, and it is not a new
problem. The New Testament contains an excellent indict-
ment of it. In that holy book, Christ castigates those in the
temple who make a great show of giving their wealth to
God, when in fact their acts are designed to gain them social
approval and status. Any time we use spirituality—whether
as a philosophy to justify our worth, a means to enhance
our reputation, or a method to obtain physical benefits—we
are practicing spiritual materialism.

Materialism of any kind involves transactions. In spiritual materialism, these form what my teacher called the "spiritual marketplace," a term that should resonate with anyone who has been sold its goods—healing crystals, trips to sweat lodges, foolproof ways into God's good graces, fancy new Buddhist practices—on radio, television, newspapers, the Internet, or in person.

Spiritual materialism is inherently repulsive, but how does it harm spirituality? Spirituality is about mind, which we can think of as a glass of muddy water. If we allow the glass to sit, the water clears; if we shake it, the water remains muddy, and we never see its transparent nature. If we agitate mind with our wants—*any* wants, including wanting to get something or somewhere with spirituality—we cloud its pristine awareness, and block our ability to appreciate its enlightened nature. If we divert mind from itself to anything, we abandon the true source of our spirituality, and risk shopping until we die without ever finding what we need.

Using spirituality in ego's service is not an easy problem to overcome, even in valid spiritual traditions. Speaking within his own tradition, Chögyam Trungpa said that we are all spiritual materialists until the moment of enlightenment. Even in the best of circumstances, materialism haunts us. No matter who we are, if we search for mind rather than simply being it, we are caught in the embrace of spiritual materialism.

There is only one authentic form of spirituality, and that is the experience of the true nature of mind. To become a spiritually authentic person, we will have to gain that experience, and to do that we must be introduced to a simple meditation practice, and to someone who prevents us from straying into materialism. These are the first milestones on the path to true spirituality, free from spiritual materialism.

CONCEPT

We might ask: if the material is presented accurately, does it really matter if a teacher has only a conceptual understanding of it?

At times, I discuss the Dharma on Buddhist Internet forums. One of the most common rebuttals in these groups is that someone lacks valid experience of a topic—that he or she is caught in concept.

Concept does indeed pose a big problem in the Dharma, and it is a problem that worsens as we continue on the path. Teachers are especially prone to confusing what they know with what they experience. For example, having discussed emptiness for many years, they may begin to feel that they have experienced it. Having been in a war, and having heard a lot of war stories, I can understand: over time, it becomes increasingly difficult to remember if what one experienced in war actually happened or was simply heard. I seldom talk about the war except with people who were there, but when I do, I make certain to avoid the trap of confusing concept with experience.

Concept is something conceived in mind or a theoretical construct about something. Anything that isn't experienced is concept. If we have not flown an airplane, anything we say about flying planes is a concept, something conceived in our mind but never actually performed. Unfortunately, it can be difficult to distinguish between concepts about the Dharma and accounts of actual dharmic experience. Unlike horse riding, where this dilemma is resolved by putting the talker on a horse and clucking, tests for realization are not so straightforward. Even in the flesh, experienced teachers can talk persuasively about fruition experiences without having had them, especially to people who also have not.

We might ask: if the material is presented accurately, does it really matter if a teacher has only a conceptual understanding of it? The problem is that the Dharma is experiential material, so someone endowed only with concept about it cannot actually present it accurately. I have listened to teachers present aspects of the Dharma they had not experienced, and no matter how persuasive and informed they were, they invariably said misleading things. The limitations of language make anything said about experience misleading to some extent, so to compound the problem with outright misinformation is truly unfortunate.

I feel for people who are being misled, because their innocence touches me. When someone has the openness and

desire to learn something and is led astray—whether inten-
tionally or not—my heart goes out to that person. Also, I
feel for myself. Dharma is what I am. I can listen calmly to
people voice varying opinions about most topics, but I have
great difficulty listening to people misrepresent what I am. I
cherish what I am, or more accurately am not. We don't like
someone mistaking our name or misrepresenting our level of
education or status in the workplace, so it's understandable
if I am sensitive about something as personal as what I am.

Being realized is like speaking a native language. No
matter how well others speak our native tongue, if they
make one mistake, we notice it. If a patient tells me, even
in perfectly inflected English, that he drank his medicine
that day, I know he is a native Spanish speaker. (In Spanish,
one does not take medicine, one drinks it.) Similarly, no
matter how well someone presents the Dharma, only one
mistake reveals that he or she is not speaking from experience. I remember hearing a teacher with credentials state
that emptiness was sharp. Feeling emptiness as many things
but not sharp, I corrected him, and he graciously accepted
my correction, recognizing that he had made an error in my
native tongue.

We cannot communicate without concepts, at least
without resorting to slaps, shouts, or silence like the Zen
masters of the past—and what modern student would tolerate that? Great teachers like mine can transmit the nature
of enlightened mind simply by their presence, but in my
experience, such beings are rare. Realistically, we are stuck

with using concept as an approximation of the experiences of the Dharma, and, in many cases, with relying on unrealized teachers to transmit it. Such teachers generally do an excellent and important job disseminating the teachings, even if they lack experience of what they teach.

Having said that, there is a way to become what the concepts point to, and that is meditation. Short of having a great teacher, meditation is the most accessible introduction to the true nature of the Dharma. It alone can show us where concept stops and experience begins. If we are willing to sit quietly and observe mind, eventually our experience of it will supersede our ideas about it, and we will have transcended the problem of concept.

Doing the Dishes

Whatever our attainment, without mindfulness
we are lost in the big city of our dreams.

On an average morning, I feed the horses, meditate in my shrine room, cook breakfast, and do the dishes. Each of these four activities should be of equal spiritual importance, but meditation has an edge because it is the only time I devote exclusively to looking at mind; the other times I'm paying attention to hay, bacon, or the egg on the silverware. Of the four, though, the best indicator of the quality of my mental state is the dishes.

Meditation shows me when I'm in the present, and it helps take me there and keep me there. With the dishes, however, I have no such support system, plus they are boring, so I continually find ways to mentally divert myself from the boredom. As a result, nothing tests the strength of my focus that day like the dishes. If I can be aware of washing the dishes for any period of time, I know my spiritual practices are working. This is a literal example of my teacher's suggestion that we stay present at the "kitchen sink" level of existence: the real, nitty-gritty world, the world of dishes, not the fantasy world of our ideas and concepts.

The term used in the Dharma for being aware of the dishes, or anything else, is mindfulness. Definitions of mindfulness abound, but the one I most prefer defines it as "filling body with mind." When body is filled with mind, we become full of mind—"mind full"—and enter the real world. When mind leaves body and becomes entangled in thoughts and emotions, we leave the real world.

So, we might ask, who needs the real world? After all, it's often filled with personal and interpersonal problems. This is true, but it's also where the hot water is. If our mind wanders while we're washing the dishes and our hand strays under scalding water, we immediately understand the merit of staying in touch with the real world. Also, in a more spiritual context, the real world is where enlightenment is. If a juicy thought steals our attention, we leave enlightenment's neighborhood. We may have crystal-clear experiences of egolessness, nonduality, and emptiness, but without mindfulness we can't access them. Whatever our attainment, without mindfulness we are lost in the big city of our dreams.

The Dharma is a very difficult discipline, but for me two aspects stand out as the most difficult: experiencing nothingness and being mindful. Most of us are easily impressed with the challenges inherent in experiencing nothingness.

Since our whole life has been involved with "something-ness," our mind must make a U-turn and see in a completely new way. With mindfulness, the problem is different: we know what to do but we can't do it, because we suffer from an addiction worse than alcohol, drugs, or cigarettes: an addiction to our thoughts and emotions. Many times each day, we leave the present to grasp tempting thoughts and persuasive emotions. Remembrances of the past, plans for the future, and emotions like anger, fear, and longing continually pull our attention away from the here and now.

To make matters worse, mindfulness can't be done. It has to happen. Using meditation, we can put ourselves in a position for mind to come back, but we can't *make* it come back, and once it is back we can do very little to keep it there. In fact, if we try too hard, mind rebels and staying in the present becomes even harder. Effort doesn't help—and therein lies the key to mindfulness. The best way to cultivate mindfulness is to relax, be kind and gentle to ourselves, and resist beating ourselves up over not being mindful.

Today, I did pretty well with the dishes. I stayed relaxed and didn't burn myself or get caught up in my thoughts, but I did think of this chapter. Did I "sin" against mindfulness in so doing? Not really. There will always be thoughts, so we have to accept them and learn to relate with them. As we progress, we will eventually begin to notice when we're thinking, and learn how to think and remain in the present at the same time. Today, I was able to that; tomorrow will be another test. There are no guarantees with a demanding spiritual practice like the dishes.

DREAMS

---

*I feel about the spiritual power of dreams
the way I feel about ghosts: I refuse to believe
in them unless they force me to.*

I hesitate to write this next entry, since it deals with a recent insight that occurred in a dream. The Dharma recommends that we keep new insights private, and not risk polluting them with our descriptions: better to stay with the experience than risk losing it in translation. Since I'm talking to myself here, I'll take the risk.

Knowing how boring other people's dreams are, I'll make this brief. In the dream, I found myself with other realized people. We were all in robes. One person looked into my eyes in passing and then away, and then again penetratingly. Wonderfully, he had seen what I truly was. We murmured greetings and I remember telling him we would talk again. I also remember standing in a group of gentle, relaxed people with knowing eyes; the feeling of being home with others like myself; and the feeling of pure bliss. In fact, the bliss itself was the insight, because by literally fulfilling my dreams, the dream uncovered the place of my bliss. When I awoke, I continued to feel it, and to know where to find it. The old saying "find your bliss" comes to mind as a description of the experience—not in the sense of discovering what causes it, but of actually finding where it resides. Despite that phrase's smarmy associations with quick-fix spirituality, finding my bliss is exactly what happened to me in, of all things, a dream. It was a miracle.

The last I read about dreams, the common dogma was that they are ways mind tries to make sense of our everyday activities. During the day, we wash the car, have an argument with our spouse, and find out that our investment planner is a crook. That night, we dream that our spouse runs away with the investment planner, and they both die when their car plunges into the ocean. I think this understanding of dreams is partially true, but insufficient to explain how dreams impart spiritual insights.

Milarepa once discussed dreams with his Dharma heir Gampopa. In the exchange, Milarepa tells Gampopa that dreams generally have no spiritual significance, then proceeds to interpret a recent dream of Gampopa's, which he finds to be loaded with spiritual import. (Go figure.) Later in his life, Gampopa has another dream where he cuts off his son's head. From then on, he never dreams again, and his sleep transforms into realization. I remember my own teacher telling us to pay attention to our dreams "because they are real," and how he often appeared in them. Spiritual dreams appear to represent more than the mundane explanation suggests.

I feel about the spiritual power of dreams the way I feel about ghosts: I refuse to believe in them, unless they force me to. I once worked in my teacher's home, where a ghost was reputed to live. While I and a fellow laborer were working there, he heard someone call his name. It wasn't me, and no one else was there, so I told him about the ghost. He accepted the news with equanimity, and we went back to work. As Hamlet said, "There are more things in heaven and earth, Horatio, than are dreamt of in your philosophy."

REAL

---

*That is the trick to being real: having
our activities come out of nothingness.*

I saw a TV ad some time ago in which a professional basketball player admonished viewers to "get real." I liked the
ad, because real appeals to me. I treasure what I have come
to recognize as the real world, and I like and respect real
people. Of the latter, though, it is sad but true that few actually exist: to a greater or lesser extent, ego forces almost all
of us to play a role. We may play the macho male, ready to
smash the world into our likeness; or the executive woman,
suited up and ready to compete; or, closer to home, the
highly skilled physician, a role that provides the background
for the following story.

In the middle of my medical career, feeling that I was
missing something important in life, I left my teaching job
and allowed life to take me where it wished. And it did, to a

Buddhist meditation center in Barnet, Vermont, belonging to my future teacher. I first met him there, on one of his visits to the center. Someone mentioned to him that I was a physician. Not caring a fig for his body (as I would later learn), but always looking to help others with his presence, he invited me to examine some problems he had with his neck and knee.

It turned out to be my own examination. Great teachers, among their many qualities, act as a mirror, and that night I observed myself in my teacher's mirror, playing the role of a doctor. In it, I watched as I enacted someone puffed up with credentials and pompously knowledgeable. The separation between what I truly was and the person I played as a doctor was there for all to see. I found myself, the examiner, examining myself in a mirror that revealed all the inauthenticities of the role I played.

Only one remedy exists for not being real: we must experience the absence of self. As long as we have an entity superimposed on the nothingness we really are, we can never be completely real. As Shunryu Suzuki Roshi said in *Zen Mind, Beginner's Mind,* "It is rather difficult to explain, but naturalness is, I think, some feeling of being independent from everything, or some activity which is based on nothingness." That is the trick to being real: having our activities come out of nothingness. We all manifest in different ways, but we will manifest authentically if we do so out of nothingness. But if our personality comes from a sense of self, from whom we think we are or should be, we will never be real.

Chögyam Trungpa acted contrary to most people's template of a spiritual person. He was married and had what the uninitiated might call affairs, and he drank to what the uninitiated might call excess. I saw him do these things. Nevertheless, whether he was in bed with a woman or staggering drunk, everything he did came out of nothingness. Everything he did was completely real, and without any hint of self-serving machinations. No matter what the circumstances, he remained authentic in every moment.

In addition to real people, there is the real world. The nature of that world can be very confusing, unless one is fortunate enough to experience it. When one does, the reason for the confusion becomes evident: the real world happens to be unreal. When we experience emptiness, it reveals the world to be an unreal place. Computers, concrete, and carnations lose their real appearance, and take on an illusory one. That is how the real world becomes unreal.

Realization makes us real people in the real world, and more: it joins the two in nonduality. With the experience of emptiness, we discover ourselves and the world to be the same. Being nothing, we exist inseparably with a phenomenal world afloat in nothing.

To become truly real, we must transcend ego's revisionism about who or what we are, and then see through the heavy veneer of realness it has projected onto the world. We then become real citizens in a spacious, joyful, and real (unreal) world that is the same as ourselves.

SPORTS

We never know how our lives will go,
and nothing demonstrates that better than
the way sports helped me in the Dharma.

At the age of seven, I was on my own in this world. That was the age at which I entered a boarding school, one of a number I would attend up through age eighteen. Since being abandoned by one's parents destroys self-esteem, I had to find ways to enhance mine. Sports, I found, were a good way. Without parents, peer approval became paramount, so I learned to impress my schoolmates with athletic prowess. I worked many hours honing my skills, particularly in baseball and basketball; my focus on sports became so narrow that I barely noticed others without athletic ability, and not until medical school did I develop friends with interests other than sports. To this day, even when the old rocking chair and TV remote have claimed many in my age group, I continue to be athletic.

We never know how our lives will go, and nothing demonstrates that better than the way sports helped me in the Dharma. Athletic disciplines may not intuitively seem to be good preparation for spirituality. In fact, I can't recall any Dharma teacher I've known extolling sports, other than a Zen teacher named Katagiri Roshi, who once used a batter concentrating to slow down a fastball as an analogy for how meditation reduces the speed of mind. I understand why sports aren't mentioned in Buddhism: after all, they're goal-oriented (at least the way I played them), and they lead to aggression (also the way I played them). Nevertheless, they have undoubtedly contributed to my progress on the spiritual path.

Sports helped me avoid a conceptual approach to Buddhism. Because of my upbringing (or lack thereof), I learned at an early age that actions speak louder than words. To talk about hitting a baseball, no matter how eloquently, isn't the same as actually hitting one. At some point, all our well-laid plans face someone standing on a mound: someone with a particular talent at throwing baseballs, eight other players around him determined to make us fail, and a plan of which we, waiting below, have no knowledge. Then, he delivers the ball, and no amount of concept can help us hit it. It's time to perform.

The experience of performing in sports greatly informed my approach to the Dharma. From the very beginning, I accepted nothing short of enlightenment as my reason for practicing Buddhism. Enlightenment was the performance aspect of the Dharma, and from my perspective everything else was talk—important talk, maybe, but still talk. That's the way I trained myself in sports, and that's the way I approached the Dharma. After many years, I am pleased with my decision.

Sports also taught me that I could accomplish my goals. I remember the first time I scored in a basketball game. I can see and feel that moment as clear as day: time stood still, I shot, and the ball went in. It was a feeling of complete affirmation. I had done it, but more importantly I had found out I *could* do it. What I found out didn't apply only to basketball, but to my whole life, including the Dharma.

I had the incredible good fortune to meet a buddha in this lifetime. The moment I saw him, I knew I had never seen anything like him, and not long afterward I saw he was living enlightenment. Although I stood in awe of him, I never forgot my experiences in athletics. He was incredible, but he was still a human, and if he could do it, so could I. Although enlightenment seemed very far away at the time, I had the foundation of all the effort I had expended developing a regular athlete into a good one. I remember how long it took me to learn to shoot a basketball with my left hand, and the pleasure I felt when I did it in a game and knew my persistence had paid off. My experiences in athletics encouraged me to "do" spirituality as well, even when I later learned that it couldn't be done.

Anyone who has ever played sports knows how difficult and disappointing they can be. Even the best batters in baseball get a hit only one-third of the time: hitting a baseball is really difficult—as only using a thin cylinder to hit a small sphere traveling at high speed can be—and becomes hellishly so when the pitchers curve the ball. Waiting for a fastball and getting a curveball, when first experienced, is like being paralyzed. The contrast between a straight and a curving ball is so shocking, so devious, and so unfair that in professional baseball a pitcher with good curving pitches is said to have "filthy stuff," the implication being that the pitcher must be morally depraved to involve himself in throwing them.

I find that curveballs in baseball are much like nothingness in spirituality. Gaining facility with the things of the world—taxes, typing, treading water—is difficult enough, but to expect us to realize the no-thingness of life is downright unfair. Trying to experience nothingness is filled with difficulties and disappointments, so it helps to have prior experiences with difficult disciplines, such as sports.

The Buddhist path requires courage. In the Dharma, we will sit for thousands of hours; attempt to act civilly when not inclined; stick our neck out in unimaginable ways for another human being called our guru; and, if we attain fruition, adhere to the truth of our experience in a world that by and large has no idea such experience exists. If we really do spirituality right, we will commit our lives to it, and that takes courage. Most importantly, we need courage to risk ourselves in the pursuit of enlightenment. After all, how can we expect to be rid of the biggest impediment to enlightenment, our self, without the courage to withstand the decline and death of that closest of companions?

As I grew older and my body started to fail, I resolved to get a new one: I bought a horse. In my fifties, I found myself participating in three-day eventing, one of the most dangerous athletic endeavors on the planet. It involves, among other things, jumping 1,200-pound animals over solid fences. "Solid" is the operative word here, because when a horse hits a fence that doesn't give, the horse gives, and the results can be fatal to the rider.

I could have pursued any number of equine sports, any of which would have been dangerous (horses are innately that way), but I picked the most dangerous one. Why? Because galloping a horse cross-country and jumping it is the biggest thrill I have ever experienced in athletics, and because I had the courage to do it. I had learned about overcoming fear as a young man facing fastballs and partisan crowds, and that courage extended to my later life as an athlete. It also extended to my approach to spirituality. Because of sports, I found the courage to supplicate my teacher in the face of the greatest adversity; to practice patiently for years, much of that time without the support of insight; and to stick my neck out far enough to get my attachment to the world cut off.

I love athletics, but not so blindly that I ignore how other disciplines also help one overcome fear and build confidence. In fact, almost all of life's endeavors, from raising children to writing a book, provide the same psychological benefits as sports if done correctly. In the final analysis, the activity doesn't matter as much as our commitment to it. If the commitment is there, all the necessary personality traits will arise as well. And no matter how we gain those traits, we will need them in spirituality, for it is a severe discipline.

Blindness

*Everyday blindness is in some sense
worse than organic blindness.*

My subspecialty in medicine is rheumatology. One of the diseases I treat, and one that causes me frequent anxiety, is temporal arteritis. Temporal arteritis is an inflammatory problem that occludes (closes off) blood vessels supplying the optic nerves, causing sudden blindness. Since both eyes may become involved, the risk of total blindness is quite real. I remember a patient of mine whose temporal arteritis had been treated unsuccessfully by another doctor: he sat in my office as if made of stone, staring vacantly into space. I felt pity for him, and for his former doctor, who if sued was in for some dark times as well. As a physician, I know something about blindness, but I know more about it as a Buddhist.

Without meditation, many of us suffer from everyday blindness. Although our eyes can still see, we have lost awareness of the world before them. When we enter a room, we fail to see the decorations on the wall or the pattern on the carpet, even though our gaze passes over them. After fifteen years, I still see houses in my neighborhood for the first time, not because they are newly built, but because I have failed to notice them. Each of the countless times my eyes have scanned them, I was occupied with something else. I was watching the soap opera in my head rather than the world before my eyes.

Everyday blindness is in some sense worse than organic blindness. With true visual loss, we lose sight of the world, but we remain aware of sound, smell, touch, and our thoughts. With everyday blindness, however, we lose everything. When we are caught in thought, the loss of awareness is so profound that we don't even know the content of the thought that occupies us: we completely black out even to thought itself, as well as to all other sensory input. It's as though we are floating in a sensory deprivation chamber.

Like everyone else, I have blacked out countless times. Fortunately, meditation has taught me to recognize when I am doing so. Also because of meditation, I'm less prone to it, which allows me to see more of what I'm looking at—including other people blacking out. I often see those eyes, opaque with the loss of observation, staring blankly at the world while their owners drift about in thoughts and emotions.

I have known only one person who never succumbed to everyday blindness, and that was my teacher, Chögyam Trungpa Rinpoche. In all the millions of moments I observed him, his awareness never strayed from the present. He saw everything that passed before his eyes. Once, an attendant saw his eyes clearly as he turned to look at a sudden disturbance, and observed that they saw everything they passed on the way to focusing on the disturbance.

Being with someone who never goes blind can be disconcerting. I recall meeting my teacher in a bookstore. When he arrived, I had just met someone recently back from Tibet, whom I introduced to Rinpoche, thinking that he might enjoy hearing some news from his homeland. While he and the traveler conversed, my mind wandered—until I awakened from my torpor to find my teacher looking directly into my eyes. It seemed he had been doing so for hours. Since I had been practicing for many years at that point, my blindness was especially embarrassing.

There are many good reasons not to go blind. The world is filled with solid and not-so-solid entities that can create problems for us. Missing a red light while thinking about a recent emotional interaction can introduce us to the solid ones, and making an ill-advised comment to a close relative or boss while blinded by anger can introduce us to the less material but more lasting and painful ones. The point is: we really can't afford to go blind in this life.

DIRECTION

We may have trouble concentrating on a single
tree in a dense forest, but if we clear a space
around that tree, we find we can see it better.

I am always amazed at how insidious concept is. I seldom recognize when I am caught in it. Only through sudden, unexpected insight do I see it, and then I'm usually puzzled at how obvious it was, or should have been. Today, I had such an insight about direction.

I have experienced the vast, limitless quality of mind for some time. Also, I have realized that its vastness is me, and not something that only exists outside the limits of my body. Until today, however, the vastness was occurring mainly in front of me, rather than all around. In retrospect, I can understand how this happened: my eyes face forward, and being a man I have no concept of a backside, a trait that will be familiar to women who see men use mirrors regularly without ever looking at their rear ends.

After the insight, as often happens, I remembered something I had read. It was a story about a Zen master and a student that followed a familiar form: the student had attained some level of insight into the nature of mind, and was testing his understanding against that of the master. In response to the student's comments, the master asked, "Where is mind when you stand on your head?" The student paused, not having reached the degree of insight probed by the question. He was caught in the concept of direction, as I had been. He had not yet realized that mind is all around, and not confined to a certain direction or spatial orientation.

This insight about direction may seem trivial, but it's not. Anything we fail to recognize about the totality of mind limits our freedom. One of the bugbears of meditation is thought's ability to steal awareness. Until we see each of our thoughts as they arise—a difficult task—they continue to interfere with our experience of mind. One way to help ourselves with this problem is to gain a better perspective on our thoughts. We may have trouble concentrating on a single tree in a dense forest, but if we clear a space around that tree, we find we can see it better. Similarly, without a spacious mind we lose perspective on each thought, but if we increase the space of mind, we are able to recognize and inspect each thought more easily. Increasing the space of mind by any means, including seeing that it is without direction, helps us do that.

This insight brings me back to meditation. Without meditation, I would never have discovered that mind has no direction, because only meditation provides the means to examine mind thoroughly. Without it, I never would have found the direction to no direction.

WRITING

---

*I write to spread the word about the most
important aspects of the human condition:
knowing who we are and what the world is.*

Writing isn't easy—notwithstanding one "how-to" author's affirmation that if you can talk, you can write. I don't talk the way I write: in everyday conversation, I never say, "Notwithstanding one 'how-to' author's affirmation." I'm more likely to say, "Even though one guy said," or something equally plebeian. I remember Kurt Vonnegut relating in an interview that he had always had great ideas, but for a long time he couldn't write well enough to bring them to the public. Another writer, Red Smith, said that writing wasn't difficult; one simply had to "open a vein"—a bon mot I find too true.

So why do I do something so difficult? Fortunately, it's not because I suffer from a need to be a great writer. In fact, I don't consider myself a writer at all. (Perhaps others concur.) My real interest is realization, and writing is simply a way to share my enthusiasm with others. I even question whether I could write about anything other than realization: besides not interesting me, creating a character or dialogue, or even writing a good travel article, may be beyond what writing skills I possess. It is fortunate, then, that I only have to observe what I am and record it.

I write to spread the word about the most important aspects of the human condition: knowing who we are and what the world is. I write about the Buddhadharma, the only discipline I know of that satisfactorily addresses these issues. Many religions believe they have successfully dealt with these topics, but I have complete confidence in the Dharma, because I experience what it teaches. I know its truths not only logically but experientially: I have not only heard that water assuages thirst, but I have drunk it and found that it does.

Even science, the basis of my practice of medicine and the only other bastion of truth I know, means less to me than the Dharma. Science tells me the truths of the physical world, but I am not truly physical: I am not really my body, but something else, just as the phenomenal world is something other than form. What I truly am is emptiness and only the Dharma addresses that fact. Because of the importance of the Dharma, people like me feel the need to share our experience with others through the cumbersome process of writing.

Most of the world believes that what we do is paramount, and much is written about what has been done, what needs to be done, and how to do it. But knowing what we *are* actually carries much more importance than knowing what to do. Furthermore, if we don't know what we are, what we do is often inappropriate. Mistakenly seeing ourselves as a "this" interacting with "that" rather than the two being one in emptiness, or the world as a rigid reality rather than form leavened by emptiness, leads to wars, pollution of our planet, and universal unhappiness. For these reasons, I persevere, writing to no one about the importance of nothing.

HEALTH

*There are times to render unto Buddha what is Buddha's
and unto Western medicine what is Western medicine's.*

Chögyam Trungpa died at age forty-eight. His early death
made not a particle of difference to him; in fact, in his last letter to us he said he was "happy to die." Before his own death,
the sixteenth Karmapa consoled a teacher of mine who was
begging him not to leave by saying, "Nothing happens."

For enlightened beings, death isn't a big deal. It should
be to us, though, if we want to attain enlightenment, because
most of us will need all the time we can get. And if we don't
do it in this lifetime, who knows what will happen in the
next (when we return as, say, a sponge)? For these reasons,
we need to preserve our health and live as long as possible.

I knew a fellow physician who decided to dedicate
his life completely to the Dharma. He quit his practice,
moved to India, and entered a lifelong retreat. They gave

him pliers to pull out bothersome teeth so he would never have to leave. They should have given him a colonoscope, because after some time he developed an advanced colon malignancy that routine colonoscopy would have diagnosed. When he returned home to die, I heard he had made excellent progress on the Buddhist path; nevertheless, he died prematurely because of his inexcusable choice not to screen himself for colon cancer. Who knows what he could have attained if he had watched his health, and lived a full life? I was angered that my friend lost his life this way: being a physician, he should have known that not even lifelong retreats grant immunity from cancer.

Spiritually inclined people commonly disregard scientific knowledge. After many years, I no longer freely advise Buddhists about medical matters: I leave them to their sweat lodges, crystals, and herbs. It is shocking to find such ignorance among a well-educated and intelligent group. I attribute it to arrogance, fortified by a correct spiritual choice that they believe carries over to physical ones. Fortunately, most medical problems are trivial in the West thanks to our level of nutrition, hygiene, and use of vaccines. On the other hand, serious diseases do occur, and treating them inappropriately despite having access to all the medical benefits of the West is, in my opinion, unconscionable.

I have reminded not a few practitioners that Tibetan monasteries in the twentieth century and before were riddled with tuberculosis as well as other diseases now curable in the West. Anyone who sees a picture of Kalu Rinpoche, a famous Tibetan teacher and tuberculosis sufferer, will observe by his cadaverous appearance the devastation disease wrought on Tibetan monks. Indeed, one would be hard-pressed to find a better venue for the spread of tuberculosis than a Tibetan Buddhist shrine room, sealed against a frigid Tibetan winter, filled with monks chanting and coughing on each other. No number of sadhanas, fire pujas, or medicine Buddha chants could do what Western medicine did in curing tuberculosis and other deadly diseases in Tibet. There are times to render unto Buddha what is Buddha's and unto Western medicine what is Western medicine's.

Will Durant, a marvelous historian, summed up in *The Lessons of History* the recurring historical themes he noted after many years of study. He labeled one of them "primitivism," a tendency of cultures to reject the progress they have made and return to older ways. Examples of this regressive tendency are seventeenth- and eighteenth-century European writers who extolled the virtues of the "noble savage," man in his "natural state," and a world stripped of the oppression of organized society. If they had starved with the Sioux (as the Sioux often did when their provisions ran out), or watched them flay an enemy to death one piece of skin at a time, I doubt they would have exchanged their lives for a native's.

In my own life, I have observed primitivism in medicine. Having the use of potent antibiotics, heart, blood pressure, and cancer therapies, and seeing ventilators and intensive and coronary care units save life daily, I was incredulous to encounter patients delaying appropriate diagnostic tools and therapies to take nostrums or apply spirituality that had failed in the Middle Ages. I was astounded to see intelligent Westerners visit Tibetan physicians, who recommended not sitting in cold places for insulin-dependent diabetes, and who assured their patients that they could stop insulin if they complied. Antiquated ideas persist: it's a historical as well as a hysterical fact.

To me, the main reason for living is to attain enlightenment. Whatever helps us to do that should be cherished, including living a healthful and long life. Mental and physical impairments complicate our search for enlightenment, and an early death excludes us from it. We need to pay attention to our health in intelligent ways and live long enough to fulfill our spiritual goals.

LIFE

*If we can control mind we can
control life, because they are the same.*

For most of us, life is a big deal, something to battle with
in the hope of being "successful." Unfortunately, most of us
have not really examined what might constitute success in
life, so we accept the models given to us—wealth, power,
successful interpersonal relationships—even though we
don't know where those models originated. If we looked,
we would find they come from a nonexistent (but insa-
tiable) creation of our mind called ego. Ego both sets the
standards for our lives and makes them too complex for
us to enjoy. If we adjust our perspective, however, we can
transcend ego's approach and experience life in a simplified
and fulfilling way.

The quickest way to recognize life's simplicity is to meet
someone totally without ego, a buddha. I have had that good

fortune. Chögyam Trungpa referred to the great simplicity of siddhas, or enlightened beings, and he knew of what he spoke. He was a siddha, and he did live simply, not physically but mentally. He had cars, homes, a wife and children, wrote books, translated religious texts, and traveled all over the world. His actions, however, were a reflection of his mind and were always quite simple. He never hurried or became overwhelmed or confused by experience, no matter how demanding situations became. He stayed completely awake and relaxed, solidly in the present, under all circumstances. Although he would laugh, sometimes uproariously, or express heartfelt sadness, emotions never removed him from the world before his eyes. He never panicked or showed any real concern that I ever witnessed. Even though chaos swirled around him, he always remained a calm eye in the storm.

How was he able to approach life in this way? He gave us many insights to help answer that question. For example, he spoke a lot about the power of speed in life and how to cope with it. Modern life moves at amazing speed, and it continues to accelerate. I remember my astonishment at how quickly the Soviet Union collapsed—I had read how other empires, such as Rome, took hundreds of years to disintegrate—and at how suddenly computers changed the way information spread. In medicine, I saw the volume of information double over shorter and shorter spans, until it became difficult to stay current in even the most circumscribed disciplines.

So how do we remain unruffled in the face of such speed? Over and over, my teacher stressed the importance of meditation, and its ability to stabilize mind and help us maintain our awareness and equanimity as we face an accelerated life. Its effects remind me of dressage, a discipline both my teacher and I appreciated. Dressage is a method for training horses to efficiently and elegantly respond to the rider. One of dressage's methods is called the half-halt, which, perhaps unsurprisingly, is half a full halt. When a half-halt is performed correctly, the horse slows, then continues to move in a more balanced and attentive way. The techniques of meditation half-halt our minds, balancing them in the present instead of allowing them to rush off at the world's speed.

My teacher also taught us the principle of "one thing at a time." No matter how fast and confusing our lives may seem, only one experience at a time occurs in mind. When we allow mind to speed up, it blurs; nevertheless, the blur is only one occurrence at a time, just as a cassette tape on fast-forward is still only one word after another. No matter how confused we become, we have the support of knowing that only one thing at a time enters mind. If we slow mind enough with meditation, we can appreciate the sequential nature of experience and simplify our life.

To live life correctly, we must also realize that life *is* mind. Nothing in experience occurs outside of mind, and nothing is separable from it: mind is experience and experience is mind. We may believe that what we mistakenly call outside events influence us, but in reality they are expressions of mind. No matter how unpleasantly the world seems to treat us, the feelings of unpleasantness arise in mind, as do the activities of the so-called outside world that engender them. As a result, if we can control mind we can control life, because they are the same.

Our life depends on our relationship to mind. If we can ride it, instead of vice versa, we can find peace and simplicity. If we realize that it is not separate from what it experiences, we can spare ourselves a lot of the bewilderment that comes from trying to manipulate what is "outside" into ways that accommodate what is "inside." When we learn what mind is and how to approach it, we will learn about life.

FREEDOM

Mind is empty, and emptiness knows no limits.

Many years ago, I attended a talk by Situ Rinpoche, one of the princes of the Kagyu lineage of Tibetan Buddhism. He opened his talk by saying that people want to be happy. At the time, this seemed naïve to me: I felt that life was much more complex than that, and I thought "joyful" would have been a better choice of words for a Buddhist talk. Some thirty years later, however, "happy" seems apt.

I have personally sought happiness for much of my sixty-seven years—depression being a great motivator—so I know its importance. After a strenuous search, I believe I have found the key to happiness: freedom. I don't mean any old freedom, but unconditional freedom, freedom that doesn't depend on escaping from anything and isn't contrasted to any kind of restriction. This kind of freedom can only be found in the experience of the true nature of mind.

Mind is empty, and emptiness knows no limits. When we experience emptiness, it acts not as a savior that liberates us from confinement, but as a discovery that transcends the very idea of confinement. Furthermore, mind has never been created or destroyed, so when we discover its freedom, we find something we can trust, beyond the impermanence that characterizes everyday life.

We can only find complete happiness through the freedom of realized mind, but how do we do that? We must discover what separates us from freedom, and remove it. It's as though every time we want to go somewhere, we have to contend with a tollbooth. The tollbooth is our sense of self and other. It is what we always have to go through to progress.

The Dharma's answer to our tollbooth problem is to show us that we are already where we want to go. Discovering on the spot that there is no us and no other is, itself, freedom.

Our belief in and adherence to the dictates of self and other exclude us from the unlimited freedom of mind. When we discover that they are mistakes of mind, and mistakes that mind has the power to correct, we will find unconditional freedom. Until then, money, power, even fulfillment through our children will not provide us with real happiness. Only mind can do that.

Mantra

I went from radio to television: I now had
not only the sound of mantra, but a picture
of emptiness to go along with it.

I had another insight recently. I'm always surprised when I do, because they are by nature unexpected, and also because as I get older and my mental acuity declines I expect new insights to decrease as well. For some reason, though, I seem to be having more rather than less as I age. They say "You can't teach an old dog new tricks," but perhaps you can if the dog has been learning them all along. In any case, this old dog keeps learning them.

The insight concerns mantra, the mental repetition of a string of Sanskrit words or syllables. *Mantra* is itself a Sanskrit word: *man-* means "mind," and *-tra* means "tool," so mantra is a tool devised to protect mind. Mantra helps with one of the most difficult aspects of the Dharma: finding ways to protect what we have realized from obscuration by thoughts and emotions.

How mantra protects mind is quite clever; assuredly a genius now hidden in the mists of time discovered it. By repeating a string of words, we occupy mind and prevent distracting thoughts and emotions from entering it. Since we create the mantra and are therefore aware of it, it does not divert our attention from the present like spontaneous thoughts do. So with mantra, at least the kind I have been given, the meaning of the words carries less importance than simply saying them. Mantra keeps mind in the present, and also reminds us of the presence of mind. It is easy to unknowingly slip out of the present, as any meditator knows, so having mantra to show us where we are is helpful.

Through the years, I have turned from time to time to a book by the ninth Karmapa called *The Mahamudra*. In it, he writes of deliberately creating thoughts as a way to help us later see spontaneous thinking. In other words, by saying something in our mind and focusing on what we make up, we prepare ourselves to recognize our native or unbidden thoughts. Mantra is a similar exercise: by focusing on the mantra, we learn to recognize the natural occurrences of mind, and prevent them from stealing our awareness.

So mantra helps in a number of ways: saying it keeps us in the present; it prevents obstructing thoughts and emotions from taking us out of the present; and it teaches us to see mind's natural occurrences when they arise. Mantra is also purported to have spiritual powers. I can't attest to these, although I may have unexpectedly experienced one with the insight I will now disclose.

While walking several weeks ago, I suddenly realized that the mantra I was saying was empty. (Earlier, I extolled doing only mindfulness-awareness meditation; but as I intimated then, I am always open to changing practices, and at this writing I am again doing visualization practice.) Of course, all sound is without physical substance, but I had failed to make that connection with mantra. With the insight, I went from radio to television: I now had not only the sound of mantra, but a picture of emptiness to go along with it. Previously, mantra had only been a means to connect with the present, where I then found realization. Now I had removed that step, and mantra took me directly to realization. I had taken another link out of the insight chain; and the fewer links it has, the more accessible it becomes.

As an aside, emptiness and realization really are as simple as I have described here. In fact, I sometimes think we should be able to get the gist of them simply by listening to music. Music has no substance; it is empty, precisely in the same way realized mind is. On the other hand, I know the difference between intellectually grasping these things and actually experiencing them. Something else must happen, something at the bone marrow level of experience the Zen tradition likes so much, for us to really understand emptiness. Although only a subtle difference exists between intellectual and experiential understanding, that subtle difference makes a world of difference to us.

Since emptiness is the basis of reality, I treasure anything that enhances my experience of it. Discovering that mantra is empty may not seem like an earth-shaking event, but it was to me because it helped streamline my access to realization—and the quicker and less convoluted anyone's access to it, the better.

AGING

---

*Age flattens out mind—it lowers our
excitement and lifts our depression.*

I grow old ... I grow old ...
I shall wear the bottoms of my trousers rolled.
Shall I part my hair behind? Do I dare to eat a
   peach?
I shall wear white flannel trousers, and walk upon
   the beach.
I have heard the mermaids singing, each to each.
I do not think that they will sing to me.

We find so much about the experience of aging in these
lovely, haunting lines from T. S. Eliot's *The Love Song of J. Alfred
Prufrock:* resignation, a sense that we and the world have lost
energy, and the indecision this loss of vigor creates in us as
we age. In a world attuned to the cult of youth, many people

might find these things sad, but I don't, because they make me feel that old age is actually the best time for the Dharma.

Age flattens out mind—it lowers our excitement and lifts our depression. It knows the subterfuge behind them, having seen the depths of despair and the heights of triumph many times. The enlarged perspective of age also reveals life to be somewhat less impressive and powerful than it initially seemed: we begin to discover that life is not all it's cracked up to be, and that things are never as bad or good as they seem. We accept with aging that the mermaids will not sing to us, and that our hopes of playing major league baseball or being a prima ballerina are over. No longer filled with those distracting energies, our minds more easily find the bliss and emptiness inherent in them.

Age also brings a sense of humor. We have seen the gods of our youth toppled, their clay feet sticking in the air. Having been disappointed over and over, we acknowledge that life is too capricious to fit into our best-laid plans. This sense of humor is a kind of giving up that brings us closer to the nature of the Dharma. And age quells passion: the fires in our mind sparked by long, shapely legs or a frank, sunny smile have been banked. They no longer obstruct our cool, clear view of what we and the world really are.

The life circumstances of old age suit the Dharma perfectly, as well. The time and effort of nurturing our young has ended. Now we have the leisure to practice and experience the Dharma, and if we started young we have the accumulated spiritual experiences of our youth to assist us.

Many people devote their lives completely to their professions or children, and find themselves lost when their work ends; but aging practitioners relish the chance to devote more time to the Dharma, and they find that their practice improves as they age. And our approaching death is the perfect goad to put our life and death into proper perspective. The lines and sags we see in the mirror portend our body's death, and dissuade us from the delusion that salvation lies in our body. The evidence is irrefutable: what we are trying to hold together will soon be cast asunder.

Of course, youth has its place in the Dharma. Its energy coupled with its lack of wisdom guarantees sudden crashes, and running into enough things hard enough can provide quick insight into the cause of pain and how to avoid it. Age makes us more cautious and robs us of the insights those hard knocks provide. The Dharma relies on youth's energy and blindness for its early breakthroughs, so youth is important as well.

However, it is aging that *feels* most like the Dharma. The lessened energy of age provides restfulness and quietude like the Dharma, and it brings us closer to the unmoving state of primordial mind. Aging also teaches us about giving up, and as Chögyam Trungpa said, "When we give up, we get it."

I once wrote that the Dharma is the best retirement policy, and I continue to feel that way. Of course, the physical world is important—starving or shivering in the rain like King Lear doesn't make for a pleasant retirement. On the other hand, if our mind is in the right place, we don't need lavish accommodations in which to age.

We also find that getting old helps undermine the major problem in our life, our belief in a self. Having given up on ego's plans over and over, we are now ready for the "big one": giving up the planner.

Feeling

We don't "do" realization; it is how the
complete extinction of all our concepts
about ourselves and the world feels.

Realization can only be felt, never figured out. We cannot guess our way to the actual experience, just as our ideas and concepts about jumping a horse never approach what it feels like to jump one. The Buddha likened the teachings about enlightenment to "opening a hand" to a child: they are only employed to capture our attention, like opening one's hand to a curious tot. It is up to us to experience what they point to.

Realization is something we feel, like happiness or sadness. Like them, it has characteristics that distinguish it from other feelings. One is a sense of vastness, of being without center or fringe. This vastness comes with joy, because it is free—not tethered or grounded by anything—as well as

stable, dependably rooted in a limitless, indestructible nothingness. Realization also feels like what we really are, so
much so that the identities we had built on a name or a
job feel badly mistaken. Furthermore, our new identity is
impervious to conceptual or physical threats: it is so real
that opinions or intellectual constructs about it no longer
threaten us, and it can't be challenged physically because
it has no components to challenge. It is completely restful:
being inseparable from what we are, it never needs adjust-
ing, and being nothing, it needs no defense.

We should be happy that realization is a feeling, because
feelings are a lot more grounded than ideas and concepts.
Ideas are like fairies flying around in our head, feelings like
cannonballs in our stomach. I'd rather store important experiences as something I feel than something I think or believe: we can forget what we believe, but never what we feel.

We should also trust our heritage: we are partly animal,
and animals are good at feeling. Horses, for example, are
very sensitive. If you hurt a horse's feelings, you can see
its demeanor change. I had a good friend, a cowboy, who
roped steers. He told me more than once about a horse he
had that got downright mad if he missed a throw at a steer.
I have had similar experiences with my own horses. I have
had thoroughbreds who, instead of becoming intimidated if
I yelled at them, looked at me with a warning not to do it
again. We live near an open space called Red Mountain that
is a beautiful place to ride: it's one of those areas I call the
"real West," which means it looks like the cowboy movies I

used to see as a kid growing up in the East. Unfortunately, our horses didn't like it from the first minute we took them there—they walked sulkily and looked at each other timidly. We never were able to bring them around: it didn't feel right, and that was that. Realization operates on this gut level of conviction, with hopefully less bemusing results.

Realization is a feeling, but how do we get the feeling? The teachings repeatedly make the point that since realization is what we are, we never need to look outside ourselves to find it. Another way to say this is that realization is a feeling, and feelings only occur within us, so looking outside for them is guaranteed to fail.

The teachings on realization fill libraries, but they share a basic tenet: in order to gain it, we have to lose something else. The first thing to lose is ego. Unless we perceive unequivocally that no entity inside us controls any aspect of us—thoughts, body, or senses—we won't feel realization. We must also lose our concepts about the world's realness or solidity, and after accomplishing those two losses, we must lose duality and see that the nothingness of ourselves and the unreality of the world are the same feeling. When we have lost all that, realization will be what is left. We don't "do" realization; it is how the complete extinction of all our concepts about ourselves and the world *feels*.

ANIMALS

A horse can be tricked into giving up its freedom
for a handful of grain, but each moment we persist
in confusion, we relinquish the limitless freedom
of our mind to wanting, rejecting, and ignoring.

I have been a horse lover all my life, and have cared for, ridden, and competed horses for many years. Every day when I walk out my back door they whinny to me, and feeding them is one of the first things I do in the morning and one of the last things at night. Horses are a passion of mine, and passions are hard to rationalize, but I do know some of the reasons why they touch my heart.

Horses are as transparent and innocent as children (whom I also love), and, like seeing a great drama over and over, their predictability never detracts from their appeal. Every time I catch a horse that runs three times faster and is infinitely stronger than me with a handful of grain, I smile.

They never get it, and each time they don't, I fall more in love with them. Also, horses are always just horses. A horse never tries to appear other than it is. I still stop and watch every time a horse rolls on the ground: it's always a pleasure to see them being completely what they are.

Some people think horses are stupid, and their willingness to trade their freedom for a handful of grain does appear unintelligent from our standpoint. But when we look at horses from a horse's perspective, we find they're not so dumb. For example, I can attest that we would not survive where wild horses do, no matter how smart we were. The lack of water, severe climate changes, and predators would kill us in a matter of days. Horses survive in these places not only because they run swiftly, have coats, and eat grass, but because of their cautious nature. An injured horse in the wild is soon a dead one, so they treat their bodies with a level of care beyond what most humans, in our sheltered existence, can understand. I once owned a horse that wouldn't walk on virgin snow unless grass was growing through it. I couldn't figure out why, until I started thinking like a horse and realized that the grass assured him the snow wasn't covering ice. I suspect he fell through the ice one time, and learned how hard it is for a big body with long legs and hard hooves to climb back out.

Like all animals, horses have mental limitations. In Buddhism, humans are understood to alternate between certain styles that inhibit them from enlightenment. These styles have been categorized as the "six realms": god, jealous god, human, animal, hungry ghost, and hell being. Each realm represents a different style of confusion: self-absorption, paranoia, passion, stupidity, a sense of poverty, and anger, respectively. So the animal realm is distinguished by stupidity, and manifests as a lack of mental flexibility. The approach to everything in the animal realm is to push ahead without regard to further possibilities, like a hamster on a wheel. This is a very stupid way to approach life, but humans as well as animals get caught in it. A horse can be tricked into giving up its freedom for a handful of grain, but each moment we persist in confusion, we relinquish the limitless freedom of our mind to wanting, rejecting, and ignoring.

My son, who has been editing some of what I write, recently opined that I should be more generous in my writing. If I were more skillful I probably would, but I find myself having to choose between truth and generosity, and I'm obliged to choose the former. Fortunately, I have the example of Chögyam Trungpa to support me in my choice. He once gave a series of talks in which he likened me and my fellow students to gorillas. He described how the Dharma took gorillas like us out of the jungle and civilized us enough to get along with and even teach other gorillas. At the time, I thought that he was joking, and didn't take his comments seriously. Now, being able to compare myself with what I was then—and at times still am—I find the joke more pointed and less amusing.

For many years, I have said that the more time I spend with horses the more I learn about humans. I think the resemblance stems from the predictability of wanting. Although humans have more far-reaching desires than horses—for example, prestige and attractiveness rather than simply food—wanting is still the common denominator of life for both species. Unless we are enlightened, our wanting, aggression, and ignorance differs little from that observed in animals. We do have an advantage over animals, however: the human realm is the only realm where one can attain enlightenment. All other realms, including the animal realm, contain mental handicaps that preclude enlightenment.

The gist is humility. We need to be humble enough to accept that as humans we have a lot to learn (and experience) in life. Until we do, in many ways we differ little from the animals we feel are inferior to us. We need to remedy that situation by living in the human realm, the only one where we can attain enlightenment and transcend our animalistic tendencies.

Thingness

*We see objects as things when we
experience the world without emptiness.*

Most of us see objects as things. To complicate this mistaken perception, only those who have seen objects without thingness understand that there is a difference between the two. Although few understand it or its alternative, thingness merits discussion, because it is pivotal to understanding realization.

To understand thingness, it helps to know how it affects objects. The following words come to mind: heaviness, realness, solidity, and meaningfulness. When seen as things, objects become overlaid with a sense of seriousness, like the heavy, dark furniture and dark rooms in the *Godfather* movies. They become ponderous, more meaningful—more worthy of respect, to push the analogy. As such, thingness places a crushing burden on people who view the world in its light, a good reason to expose it for the hoax it is.

We see objects as things when we experience the world without emptiness. Without that insight, the world appears covered in concepts, among them thingness. With the experience of emptiness, on the other hand, the world changes in an instant to form: form is how objects appear in emptiness. It is as though all the Greek statuary in a museum suddenly became light and airy and rose slightly from their pedestals.

It is a great relief to observe the world without thingness. As phenomena become lighter they help us to "lighten up," to use an old Western term with a lot of Eastern insight. (Incidentally, Buddhist literature often uses the term "phenomena" to refer to objects in the world—a reflection of the way insight shows them to be less solid or real.) When the meaning and realness drains from objects, we feel less oppressed by them. The tree in our front yard no longer presents as a solidly existing thing, but as a delightfully light, unreal form, floating ever so slightly in emptiness.

It is common knowledge that we are obsessed with things. Some men's approach to life has been characterized as, "the guy with the most toys wins." All of us have a whole lot more things now than humanity did for the millennia preceding us—even the most poverty-stricken areas of the third world have cell phones and TV antennas. Moreover, our things increasingly change our lives to conform to them. The car created suburbia and the commuter culture, elevating itself from a convenience to a necessity.

We have a second obsession with things, however, one much more profound than the first and strengthened by our unawareness of it. It is our creation of thingness: our habit of saddling phenomena with a realness they don't really possess. Moment to moment, we change a delightfully light and vivid display of form into dull, heavy things. Life is difficult enough without living in a world burdened by thingness. Whether we are men or women, it's time we started seeing our toys as make-believe.

RENUNCIATION

Life is sneaky. We enter the game for a dime,
and soon find the stakes jump to a dollar.

I recently saw an eighteen-year-old boy with joint pains. His medical workup determined that he had systemic lupus erythematosus without major organ involvement, the kind we call "skin and joint" lupus. To make a long story short, his mild initial diagnosis quickly degenerated to aggressive lupus involving almost every organ in his body, and I was left holding a large bag of guilt about his poor result. Although there is much to say about his case medically, it is the Dharmic implications that prompt this entry.

As the Buddha said, "Life is pain," and I experienced considerable grief and worry over my patient's problem. Because I suffer from major depression, stress can balloon into intense worry and an inability to sleep or eat. If it persists and I am unable to stop its momentum, it begins dragging me toward suicide. At these times, I need help fast.

In this case, help came from my discovery of another one of the Buddha's truths, known as renunciation. At some point, the pain I felt, and the danger it posed, led me to simply renounce my feeling of blame—to just drop it. In the Buddhist scriptures, one finds stories of practitioners who renounced worldly concerns "like dropping a large poisonous snake." This vivid description seems like hyperbole until one grasps the snake of depression and feels the immediacy of one's danger: one must either let go or die. Thirty-five years of reading the Dharma doesn't impress one like actually holding the snake in one's hands, hearing it hiss, and seeing it prepare to strike. I held the snake and I quickly found renunciation.

The Dharma lists eight major preoccupations that distract us away from the empty awareness of realization. Known as the "eight worldly concerns," they include: gain and loss, pleasure and pain, praise and blame, and fame and infamy. They occupy us in the everyday world, and keep us from experiencing the mind of all the buddhas. In my case, because of depression, they pose a threat to my life as well.

Life is sneaky. We enter the game for a dime, and soon find the stakes jump to a dollar. We believe we can keep them low, but they keep getting higher until we either get out or go broke. Getting out is renunciation—not renunciation of our life or job, but renunciation in our approach. If we wish to find peace in this life, we must drop the eight worldly concerns from moment to moment, or the snakes of the modern world—drugs, alcohol, insanity, whatever our poison—will strike.

I assume that all Buddhists at one time or another consider living a monastic life, yearning for the peace and quiet, the chance to spend time with their mind in meditation, and the progress along the path monasticism promises. All great teachers extol the virtues of such a life, but there is also something to be said for finding one's enlightenment in the "dusty world." At times, only the stresses of a worldly life can show us the meaning of the teachings. Only when we venture to the brink of the cliff do we appreciate the wisdom that can prevent us from falling. I am a physician devoted to my patients' welfare, and I serve their needs to the best of my ability, but not to the point of accepting life-threatening blame. That is extra, dangerous to me and unhelpful to my patient, and it must be renounced. The stresses of a challenging life have taught me that.

To see what needs to be seen, we must renounce not only what we find painful, but also what we enjoy. It is easier to give up pain than pleasure: devoting our lives to praise or fame diverts our minds from enlightenment as effectively as suffering blame or infamy, and we will likely feel less urgency to remedy it. The real purpose of renunciation is to clear our minds so they can discover the enlightenment they are. Anything that obstructs mind, whether painful or pleasurable, is problematic.

Although I used renunciation to keep sane, I found more than sanity. We may be dealing with a specific problem, as I

was with blame, but in some sense renunciation is not selec-
tive: when we assume the attitude of renouncing whatever
obscures our mind, we may find ourselves giving up things
we hadn't planned to. During the past twelve years, I have
used many techniques to stabilize realization, one of which
was to connect with the illusory nature of the phenomenal
world. With the renunciation of the blame I felt, I unexpectedly found a greater renunciation that connected me to the
illusory world. Suddenly, my world became the realized view
continuously, without any need to seek for it. The effort I
had put into renunciation, spurred by my need to deal with
a dangerous depression, brought me to an unexpected and
wonderful result. I wonder if I could have applied such effort and obtained such a result under any other circumstance,
which points again to the power of worldly life on the path.

Without realization, rigidly applying the Buddhist teachings—even those on generosity, patience, or renunciation—
can lead to problems. Of course, we have to make a start before experiencing the insight of realization, but we must be
careful not to cause more harm than good in the meantime.
Once we see the nature of reality and have that basis for our
decision making, we will find that the teachings help us sustain our insight, and we can test their value by how well they
do it. This is how I experienced the real meaning and value
of renunciation, as moment to moment it took me from a
poisonous depression to the bliss of insight.

No Guarantees

The greatest failing of students of the
Dharma is an unwillingness to practice.

No guarantees exist in the Dharma. Practicing it is not like going to school: we cannot simply dedicate a given amount of time, fulfill certain requirements, and expect to automatically attain its fruitions. In fact, even after many years of diligent practice and study, many students do not receive their realization diploma.

The Dharma is very cold this way. I once read that even in the great monasteries of Japan, only one in a thousand monks experienced the full truth of the Dharma. These were men who devoted their lives to it.

Why write this? Why discourage people, when the path to realization can be discouraging enough? I write this mainly to warn against becoming complacent in the Dharma, against feeling that by simply being a Buddhist one will eventually find fruition. If we wish to succeed on the Buddhist path, we must approach each day of our lives as a precious opportunity to learn and practice.

The greatest failing of students of the Dharma is an unwillingness to practice. No matter how long we have been Buddhists, if we practice intermittently or not at all, we will never develop a good experiential understanding of the Dharma. In fact, after many years, we may be worse off than non-Buddhists, since we will have accumulated a head full of erroneous ideas about Buddhism, unsupported by insight. Shunryu Suzuki Roshi's book *Zen Mind, Beginner's Mind* alludes to this problem in its title. If we wish to progress, we must keep the fresh mind of a beginner, and that is only possible when regular meditation continually cleanses our minds of encrusted concepts.

In my opinion, the most disheartening aspect of the Dharma is how long we must practice it to experience fruition—if we ever do. In my case, having a lot of psychological pain from the outset, I did not want to wait thirty or forty years for realization to bring me relief. Expecting each moment that the Dharma would help me, I actually risked my life for ten years with untreated major depression. Fortunately, I finally made my own diagnoses and received appropriate therapy, but it would have been much nicer if I had received the help I was hoping for after sitting in meditation for a day or two. That doesn't happen. The sustained effort over years and years the Dharma requires may appeal to some people's Japanese side—just as they may find something intriguing about training for ten years to cut sushi properly—but to me it is a major drawback.

I am a fruition-oriented Buddhist. I came into the Dharma for the sole purpose of attaining enlightenment, and I have the same attitude now that I had thirty-five years ago. Nevertheless, I must mention that there is another approach to the Dharma. This approach focuses on the path to enlightenment, rather than the destination, for "the path is the goal," to quote the title of my teacher's book. In truth, the path is all there is at hand: the rest, including enlightenment, is only a dream. The truth can only be found on the path. Nevertheless, the path will not lead most of us to realization for a very long time, if ever. The path is the goal in the sense that paying strict attention to it will bring us to our destination more quickly, but not in the sense that we have arrived at that destination the moment we step on it.

We should also know that the path does provide benefits other than enlightenment. Dharma practitioners see the world and their minds more clearly—though not necessarily the true nature of either—and they learn ethical guidelines. Many times I have been impressed by the conduct of Buddhist monks. Seeing their gentleness, humility, and kindness is as great a teaching to me as those on insight. If the conduct they demonstrate was all the Dharma gave to this world, it would be enough.

In one Zen chant, practitioners vow never to stop trying to attain enlightenment, even though it is impossible to do. I've always wondered if this was a play on words, since in truth one cannot *do* enlightenment; it happens. In any case, the determination evident in that chant is the spirit of those who become realized. Even though it can't be done, they do it. It's the will that matters. I have emphasized the difficulty of reaching the destination, but that will not deter those with big hearts. Nothing can stop them from attaining enlightenment in this lifetime.

Conclusion

The true nature of mind is vast, empty,
and unchanging. If we see what arises in it
against that background, we can free ourselves
from the psychological dramas that oppress us.

Buddha's first teaching was that life is pervaded with suffering. Over forty years as a physician, I saw the truth of this teaching in my patients. Although they came to me with physical ailments, I nevertheless saw how much of their suffering was psychological, as they wrestled with their fears about losing their independence, becoming a burden to others, being unable to afford their healthcare, or facing their own death or the death of loved ones. Of course, they shared their joys with me as well: their delight in their children, in the beauties of the natural world, in their hard-earned successes. Still, they knew that no matter how well their lives went, at some point, without any previous experience to guide them, they would have to face death.

It is not unusual that my patients' minds caused them at least as much trouble as their bodies. In fact, if we truly know mind, we will see that all discomfort, including physical discomfort, arises in it. For that reason, it behooves us to understand mind, and to make a relationship with it and with what occurs in it. The true nature of mind is vast, empty, and unchanging. If we see what arises in it against that background, we can free ourselves from the psychological dramas that oppress us.

In order to see mind, we will have to give up the deeply-rooted tendencies that obscure it. We must learn how to give up—and we must not give up until we do. I hope this book has helped you determine what must be given up, where you are in that process, where you have yet to go, and how you can go there.

I also entreat you, as my teacher entreated me, to persist in meditation practice. As the great Tibetan saint Milarepa and his dharma heir, Gampopa, were preparing to part for the last time, Milarepa told Gampopa that he had one last teaching to give him, the most important teaching of all. In gratitude, Gampopa prepared to make a ritual offering, but Milarepa said "No," turned, and raised his robe, showing Gampopa the thick calluses on his buttocks from many years of sitting meditation. He said, "This is the most profound teaching in Buddhism: practice!"

Every one of us can realize the true nature of mind and reality, and enjoy the boundless freedom and richness such insight brings. It has been done in the past, it is being done now, and it will be done in the future. I hope this book has instilled confidence that realization is not some occult or mystical happening, but the result of looking with the correct guidance at mind until we ascertain its true nature. I remember fondly the times my teacher encouraged us on the path, saying, "You can do it." I believed him, and I followed his instructions. Now, some twenty-five years after his death, I can assure you as well, and with best wishes: "You can do it."

Glossary

absolute truth: The truth of the nature of mind and reality: empty, and composed of awareness undivided into perceiver and perceived.

bodhisattva: A practitioner who has made a formal commitment to attain buddhahood in order to benefit others. This vow marks the entry into the second of the three Buddhist "-yanas" or vehicles, the Mahayana.

buddha: A person who has attained enlightenment. "The Buddha" refers to the historical Buddha, Siddhartha Gautama.

Chán: See *Zen.*

confusion: The source of suffering in Buddhism. Confusion refers both to basic ignorance about the nature of reality, and to the misguided psychological states, such as passion (wanting) and aggression, that result from that ignorance.

Dharma: (Sanskrit, "truth" or "the way of things") The body of Buddhist teachings.

duality: The habitual division of experience into a subject, self, or "experiencer," and an object, other, or "experienced." A major obstacle to realization.

egolessness: The lack of any inherent existence. Sometimes divided into egolessness of self and other, pointing to the truth that no self or ego exists in oneself and that no abiding essence exists in phenomena.

emptiness: A pivotal insight occurring when egolessness of self and other are seen to be the same, indistinguishable in their feeling of absence. Along with awareness, emptiness is a basic characteristic of realized mind.

enlightenment: The permanent exhaustion of confusion—such as the mistaken belief in a self or in the reality of phenomena—resulting in bliss and limitless, uncontrived compassion for others.

form: The phenomenal world as it appears, as well as the naked experience of thoughts and emotions. All form occurs in emptiness, and when emptiness is experienced, form is seen to lack any inherent existence or reality. At the most advanced level of insight, form is seen not only to occur in emptiness, but to be it.

Hinayana: (Sanskrit, "narrow vehicle") The first of three major stages of the Buddhist path. The Hinayana practitioner concentrates on attaining personal liberation from suffering.

karma: (Sanskrit, "action") The cycle of cause and effect caused by acquired psychological predispositions that lead to habitual patterns of behavior.

Karmapa: The spiritual leader of the Karma Kagyu school of Tibetan Buddhism. The first Karmapa, Dusum Khyenpa, was born in AD 1110, and was the first Tibetan Buddhist teacher to foretell where and when he would be reincarnated. Each subsequent Karmapa has been the previous Karmapa's reincarnation.

ignorance: Not knowing the true nature of reality. Ignorance is the basis of confusion and suffering.

Mahasiddhas: Enlightened beings who epitomize the tantric (Vajrayana) principle of compassionate action completely freed from the conventions of ego. Because of this freedom, they are in touch with the magical possibilities of the world.

Mahayana: (Sanskrit, "great vehicle") The second of three major stages on the Buddhist path. Mahayana practitioners commit themselves to working for the benefit of others.

Mantra: (Sanskrit, "mind tool" or "mind protection") Sanskrit words or syllables, which are mentally repeated to protect the mind from distraction by discursive thoughts and emotions. Mantras are also concise reminders of various spiritual energies, such as compassion.

mindfulness: Sustained, undistracted attention.

realization: The direct experience that the true nature of mind is emptiness suffused with awareness. Mind has no nature: it is ineffable, intangible, and impossible to locate. At the same time, it is aware. Realization is the culmination of a series of insights into the true nature of reality. Fully stabilizing it constitutes enlightenment.

relative truth: The truths pertaining to the world as conventionally perceived. This perception is flawed by duality, and by the incorrect beliefs in a self and a world that is real.

sadhana: A spiritual text; a liturgy.

sangha: The community of Buddhist practitioners.

siddha: A practitioner who has attained *siddhis* (Sanskrit, "perfections" or "attainments"), which could include supernormal powers over the conventional world, as well as enlightenment itself. Often used to describe an enlightened person.

sitting meditation: Another term for mindfulness-awareness (Sanskrit *shamatha-vipashyana*) meditation. A practice in which one sits and pays particular attention to something, such as the breath, while being aware of the larger psychological space surrounding it.

Vajrayana: (Sanskrit, "indestructible vehicle") The third of three major stages of the Buddhist path. Vajrayana practitioners develop advanced skills for bringing others to enlightenment.

yogin: A practitioner of Vajrayana Buddhism who spends long periods of time intensively meditating in caves or other isolated places.

Zen: The Japanese pronunciation of *Chán,* a Mahayana tradition of Buddhism noted for the directness and rigor of its methods for discovering one's true nature. Chán originated in China in the fifth century CE, and later spread to Japan, Korea, and Vietnam.

Bibliography

Chang, Garma C. C. *The Hundred Thousand Songs of Milarepa*. New York: Oriental Studies Foundation, 1962.

Dorje, Wangchuk. *The Mahamudra: Eliminating the Darkness of Ignorance*. Dharamsala, India: Library of Tibetan Works and Archives, 1978.

Durant, Will, and Ariel Durant. *The Lessons of History*. New York: Simon & Schuster, 1968.

Eliot, T. S. "The Love Song of J. Alfred Prufrock." Edited by John Wain. *The Oxford Anthology of English Poetry: Blake to Heaney*. Oxford, England: Oxford University Press, 1990.

Halberstam, David. *The Best and the Brightest*. New York: Ballantine Books, 1972.

Meyer, Fred H. *In the Buddha's Realm: A Physician's Experiences with Chögyam Trungpa, a Modern-Day Buddha*. Bloomington, IN: Xlibris Corporation, 2002.

Namgyal, Takpo Tashi, trans. Lobsang P. Lhalungpa. *Mahamudra: The Quintessence of Mind and Meditation*. Boston: Shambhala Publications, 1987.

Stewart, Jampa Mackenzie. *The Life of Gampopa*. Ithaca, NY: Snow Lion Publications, 1995.

Suzuki, Shunryu. *Zen Mind, Beginner's Mind: Informal Talks on Zen Meditation and Practice*. Trumbull, CT: Weatherhill, 1970.

Trungpa, Chögyam. *Born in Tibet*. London: George Allen & Unwin Ltd., 1977.

————. *Cutting Through Spiritual Materialism*. Boston: Shambhala Publications, 1973.

————. *Shambhala: The Sacred Path of the Warrior*. Boston: Shambhala Publications, 1984.

————. *The Myth of Freedom and the Way of Meditation*. Boston: Shambhala Publications, 1976.

————. *The Path is the Goal: A Basic Handbook of Buddhist Meditation*. Boston: Shambhala Publications, 1995.

————. "The Sadhana of Mahamudra." From *The Collected Works of Chögyam Trungpa, vol. V*. Boston: Shambhala Publications, 2004.